SURVIVAL IN PARADISE

The true story of surviving a tropical storm and remote deserted
island in the middle of the Indian Ocean.

by

GORDON S. BRACE

Dedication

Dedicated to my family and many friends who eased the way
and all the adventurous souls unafraid to reach for their dreams.
Keep those dreams alive.

Contents

Foreword

January in Central Indiana is not desirable for the weather or any other events. Outdoor activities occur in a desperately cold, frozen environment, suited for only the hardiest souls; cold injuries are not uncommon. My trip from Florida to Indiana compounded negativity because I was traveling to attend my father's funeral after an agonizing five-year decline in health.

My father was a mountain of a man, whose entire identity centered around a trip to Alaska when he was twenty years old. His Alaskan safari with his brother and grandmother involved towing a ten-foot Airstream trailer, exploring America's newest state. My father's role in this adventure was a match with his fascination for the Alaskan brown bear. The Alaskan bear is not an animal to be trifled with, and the bruin mirrored my father in personality and appearance. His mastery at storytelling and desire to always outdo the last safari trip kept me on a lifelong pursuit of greater and more intense life adventures.

My first real adventure was not in the tropical climate of the Indian Ocean like Gordon Brace's story, but on a partially frozen lake where a wind shift left our seventeen-foot open boat trapped between ice flows. Herculean efforts by my father and me, with our oars, a shovel, and thirty-horsepower Evinrude, proved fruitless. A long, cold night trapped in the middle of a massive lake appeared to be our fate. Fortunately, a shift in wind and a little more effort freed us from the ice flows. Nature has its own ways, and we often find ourselves subject to those forces outside our control: strive to survive or be subjected to the wild and die. Gordon was the survivor that thrived in his environment.

After my father's funeral, surrounded by his brothers and my cousins, we decided to make the pilgrimage to the Indianapolis Sport and Travel Show. The sportsman's Mecca of Indiana, my father was the self-appointed leader of this annual foray to gather brochures, talk to outfitters, and plan the next adventure for that year. Canadian fishing trips, the western Rocky Mountains, or any other fancy that was tickled by the desire to break away. So, the gaggle of boisterous middle-aged men crashed the doors of the Indianapolis Colosseum to browse outfitters and peek into luxurious travel campers and boats.

Having read virtually every Peter Hathaway Capstick, Robert Ruark, and even Theodore Roosevelt book on Africa, my curiosity and need to take the African Safari were deeply embedded, although suppressed by always thinking the African Safari was the realm of super-rich celebrities and businessmen. At this point, I made my way alone around the show. I saw the display for Zulani Safaris, intrigued, I approached the booth just to see how far out of reach such a trip would be. Picking up the fantastic full-color brochure, perusing the photographs, Gordon approached. Khaki-clad, with a neatly trimmed scruff beard and piercing gray-blue eyes, Gordon started talking to me in his mottled African dialect.

Immediately intrigued by Gordon, I wanted to pepper him with a million questions, not necessarily about the safari, but Africa in general, and most especially who he was. Gordon projected a deep intensity that immediately grabbed the conversation and left a listener wanting to know more. Gordon exhibited the hardship, success, and striving in the most amazing environments that the average man can only read about. I have circumnavigated the globe, fought in two wars, and participated in a few skirmishes in between, and I was completely engulfed in the first conversation. Every success and failure showed in the eyes and face of this African.

After discussing prices and options of my safari and schedules, all of a sudden, Africa seemed possible. As I began to depart from an obviously busy man, I asked, "I can't place your accent, where are you from?" Gordon straightened his posture, standing to his full height, "I'm African!" "Ahh, I had just finished reading Frederick Courteney Selous's biography. I'm interested to hear more about your time there." Gordon then promised campfire conversations if I were to come to Africa. I don't think Gordon knew at this time, but he had me sold.

Two years later, I'm landing at a basic asphalt landing strip at Polokwane airport in Limpopo, South Africa. A couple of hours' drive and I'm meeting Gordon for the second time, where he greeted me with an upward grip handshake and a hug, welcoming me to Africa and Zulani. Gordon was on his way to caring for some animals, so still punchy from two days of travel and confinement on aircraft, I asked if I could help, and he readily accepted. We climbed into a vintage 1970 Toyota Land Cruiser, which could have had B.C. as the suffix to the manufacture date from the appearance of the vehicle. I can only say the Land Cruiser was a magnificent-looking beast.

Meeting Gordon in his environment convinced me the man is the real deal, a real African to his very soul, and wears his wrinkles and scars as a war hero wears his medals on Veterans' Day. Gordon's adventures are not contrived vacations booked by luxury travel agencies or manufactured by the selection of a travel brochure; his adventures were merely the process of living, existing, and surviving in environments about which most only read.

As I read the book, I can see Gordon retelling this story at the campfire, with a distant look in his eyes as he recalls a most extraordinary story. I'll never fail to be impressed by the level of hardship that is not by design or scheduled in a posh travel office but is a way of life in the African bush or on a remote tropical island in the Indian Ocean. Most of all, I'm fascinated by the easy pleasure Gordon and Elisabeth take from the simple adventure of their lives.

Captain David Hart
USMC Retired

Map of the Indian Ocean

Chagos Archipelago

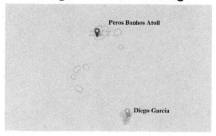

**Shipwreck trio saved after 82 days on island. 28 March 1981
Robinson Crusoe reunion. Amazing sea rescue saga of some
lucky castaways. 15 April 1981**

London Daily Express

*From left to right, Nicole Hascoet, Gordon Brace and Elisabeth
Brace*

Just One of Those Days

"How on earth did you manage to get yourself stranded
on a desert island?"
"Oh, it was just one of those days."
"Typical. It could only happen to you two!"

A conversation my wife Elisabeth and I had with a close friend soon after we arrived back in civilization. Our experience was of course far from being "just one of those days," despite our friend declaring the fact that we had been stranded on an uninhabited island in the middle of the Indian Ocean was somewhat typical of us.

In 1954, I was born in Northern Rhodesia (now Zambia). My mother, who had also been born there, was a schoolteacher, so she believed in the value of schooling. But for those days, she was a lady way ahead of her time, for she also believed in the Mark Twain maxim: not to let her child's schooling interfere with her child's education. She taught me to read and write even before I went to school, so at the young age of five, I was already somewhat ahead of my peers in the classroom.

At that tender age, my mother one day offered to send me on a three-week trip to a holiday farm in a neighboring country. I jumped at the chance. It was my first travel adventure, and I had an absolute blast! And it set the tone for my lifestyle to come.

Every aspect of the trip was organized and safe. However, upon my return from the excursion some people in our town voiced their disapproval due to my young age. My mother, as one who certainly would not to be told how to raise her child (bless her!), asked me every year afterward whether I would prefer a gift for Christmas and birthdays, or if I would instead prefer to travel - within her means, of course. No brainer. I wanted to see the world! Granny could buy the bicycle (I was no fool).

As it transpired, my grandparents got on board with this idea. The following year, they took me out of school, and together we embarked on a grand travel adventure - a major trip for anybody back then, let alone a six-year-old boy. We began the journey cruising the entire east coast of Africa aboard the *Kenya Castle*, a steam turbine ocean liner. (There was not much in the way of stabilizers back then, so we had to develop sea legs quickly - after several bouts of throwing up, I recall.) We traversed the Suez Canal, and stopped over in the Middle East, where I climbed aboard my first camel. Then we spent time in the Mediterranean and stopped over in Las Palmas and Tenerife, two of Spain's Canary Islands. Later, we disembarked at South Hampton, England and traveled up to London. After staying there for a while, my grandfather and I both went to visit his homeland - Scotland.

On the return trip to Africa, we disembarked on the shores of Kenya, where we were met by my aunt, uncle, and cousins who had a cattle and coffee farm there. While visiting here we spent quite some time at the Kenyan Coast. It was there that I was given a diving mask for the first time and explored a coral reef.

Mask in hand, 6-year-old Gordon preparing to explore the corals off the coast of Kenya.

Underwater, I couldn't believe what I was seeing: the array of colors, corals, and marine life astounded me, and they still do to this day. It was then that my love for the ocean was born, and I sought out dive spots all around the globe. (It saddens me that the array of colors and variety of formations I saw back then are now reduced to gray rubble in many coral gardens I see today, because of damage that most scientists claim is due to climate change.) After spending some weeks in Kenya with my family, I returned home with my grandparents to Northern Rhodesia (Zambia) overland via Serengeti, Tanzania, and Malawi. I remember being wide-eyed at the impressive sight of the massive herds of the wildebeest and zebra migrations there, and the predators that shadowed them. I also vividly remember one day being amazed by the sky turning pink with thousands of flamingos in flight. My love affair with the wild places and wildlife was now as passionate as my wonder of the underwater world. By the age of eighteen, I had already traveled much of Europe but more so the Sub-Saharan African Bushveld and coastlines to satisfy my love for the wild places and my passion for diving tropical gardens. I had by then spent much of my life under African stars, hunting and fishing among the wildlife there, and free diving off various places on the African coastline. However, with my school days over, new and wider horizons beckoned, along with romantic tales of tropical coral reefs that sparkled like jewels in tranquil blue and green waters. So, I skipped University, left my home in

Zambia and spent the next ten years searching for some of these wonders of the world.

A year after leaving home my wanderings brought me to Denmark, where I was first introduced to the stimulating world of scuba diving in the North Sea, searching for ancient shipwrecks. It was also there where I met a beautiful young lady, Elisabeth. She was one of those ladies who anyone couldn't help but love within minutes of meeting her. The two of us fell in love and were married a while later. Elisabeth had (and still does have) a fascination for all the wonders the world has to offer. We made a superb team together, planning and chasing many of these wonders, nearly always managing to seek out the sunny places once we felt winter nipping at our heels.

This led us from the icy North Sea to the tropical waters of the Caribbean on one of our travels. There, we made a modest living by diving for black coral, seashells, and lobsters. On one occasion, we barely survived a storm out at sea in one of the local divers' flimsy boats. To my delight, Elisabeth, instead of being deterred by this frightening escape, was excited to experience more - and more was to come.

Later I took my new wife cruising down the west coast of Africa. We traveled by train from Cape Town up to Zimbabwe, where Elisabeth fell in love with the wild places of Africa. We often sat alone together, listening to the roars of lions or the cry of the fish eagle as we watched many sunsets over many African rivers, the Kafue, Lundi, the Fish River Canyon, and Zambezi. We rafted the best white water in the world below Victoria Falls; explored the ancient Zimbabwe ruins; fished off the Skeleton Coast of Namibia; and conducted many safaris in reserves such as Okavango, Luangwa Valley, and the national parks of Kruger and Etosha. We traveled to the Cape, the most southern tip of Africa, where I fished and dove commercially for a living. Here we had a delightful episode working for a time with dolphins. Then we headed north to climb to the glacier on top of Kilimanjaro (I have that T-shirt).

Even farther north, Elisabeth and I were mesmerized by the stunning beauty of the coral and marine life below the Red Sea (where I nearly saw my end in a deep-water canyon dive). Then we traveled much farther north to the Arctic Circle, where we camped beside waterfalls overlooking fjords in the "fairyland" mountains of Norway. We made many friends across Europe. Some we joined on sailboats on the Greek Islands, lazed in the sun with on the Costa Brava, and enjoyed duty-free wines at the sidewalk cafés of Las Palmas. The songs of British pubs are not unfamiliar to us.

We traveled across the ocean to Australia, where we worked huge tractors, plowed the unforgiving land of the outback, and, of course, marveled at one of the true wonders of the world: the Great Barrier Reef. Travel, like most things of course, has its cons along with the pros, but either way, Elisabeth and I would always find our experiences to be rewarding. I have always felt somewhat indestructible. Although, like anyone, I do not like to fail, I have always lived with the philosophy of not being afraid of failure but more afraid of what I might miss out on if I did not at least try. I don't want to die wondering, "What if?" So, at times I have pushed the envelope more than a little, and Elisabeth has always supported this and even trusted it. This consequently resulted in more than a few harrowing exploits along the way. Our friend, of course, knows us and our many adventures well, and perhaps if you did, too, and are something of a fatalist like our friend is, you may also say that our adventurous lifestyle had led us to being stranded on an uninhabited, deserted island in the middle of the Indian Ocean was somewhat typical of us. You may also go on to say that this lifestyle, along with fate, led us to what is known as the "gem of Asia." The island of Sri Lanka.

Prior to arriving in Sri Lanka, we had planned to return to St. Lucia in the Caribbean. We had spent some time there, diving with the locals and taking tourists to dive spots. This resulted in us meeting someone there who offered us the opportunity to run the water sports section of a new holiday complex that was being built on the island. While this was a few months away from being operational, we returned to Denmark for a while and awaited our recall.

When word came, we headed for London from Copenhagen in transit to the Caribbean. Perhaps serendipitous, we attended a trade fair while in London to kill time and chanced upon the Sri Lanka exhibit. It captured my interest immediately, with its stunning beaches, exotic places, and rich history mixed

GORDON S. BRACE

with several cultures. The "gem of Asia" seemed to be an apt description. What also caught my eye, however, was that the exhibit claimed that Sri Lanka boasted the most inexpensive fishing boats to be found anywhere in the world.

We had never before considered going to Sri Lanka, but as I have always wished to own my own boat, this information lingered in my mind like bait on a hook. However, we had committed to going to the island of Saint Lucia in the Caribbean, which undoubtedly was a wonderful opportunity for us, and really did suit our lifestyle. The day after arriving in London, we heard some troubling news. Hurricane Allen, which was considered one of the worst on record, was headed for the Caribbean with Saint Lucia directly in its path. The following day, we heard from a news broadcast that the island we were headed for had been totally destroyed. Almost every building, plantation, and coconut palm had been flattened. Even the coral reefs had been seriously damaged. We hastily sent a message to our contact (who was in the USA) regarding the offer to run the water sports operation. We received a telegram in response:

"Extensive damage to property - operation on hold till further notice - Do not travel - will send mail - stay in touch."

On the one hand, we counted our blessings that we had missed being caught in the hurricane ourselves by just a couple of days. On the other hand, this left us stranded in London without knowing what to do or where to go.

We had previously been invited by some friends we had met in the Caribbean while they were holidaying there, to visit their home in England. They actually lived in Ascot close by to where we were staying in London - only about an hour away. So, we took them up on their invitation. We were warmly welcomed into their home with a hearty meal waiting for us. They wanted to know all about our latest adventures. We relayed to them our recent dilemma, only to find that they had something of a surprise for us—they had just returned from Sri Lanka themselves! Was this a coincidence? Or, perhaps, was this more of a nudge from fate?

For most of the evening, they couldn't enthuse enough about Sri Lanka. Before we went off to bed, it seemed the Sri Lankan bait that was dangling before me had me well and truly hooked. The following day, Elisabeth and I made inquiries about heading for the "Gem of Asia," and requested more information regarding the purchase of a boat there.

Back then, there were warnings not to fly the Soviet airline Aeroflot. Despite this, we decided that we would chance it, as it was the cheapest way to go. It was quite a journey.

We did not realize there were no seating allocations on the plane, and we were wondering why all the passengers were running to the stairway. We boarded, only to find there were not enough available seats for us to sit together, and no one would change to accommodate us. When we asked the hostess if she could help us, she scowled at us and growled something that had us wondering who the customer on this flight was. So, we had to sit separately all the way to Moscow. The food we were served was something akin to cardboard even by airline standards.

This was during the height of the Cold War, so when we disembarked in Moscow, everybody there was scowling at us decadent Westerners, as though we were directly responsible for all their problems. We were stuck in this cold, friendless airport for sixteen hours, waiting for our next connection. When the time came to depart, we left through the metal detectors. My belt buckle set off the alarm, and the immediate aggressive reaction from the officials had me backed up, thinking, *Oh, hell. Siberia, here I come!*

This time, though, when we were about to board the plane, I ran ahead and spread my elbows at the stairway to allow Elisabeth to climb under my arms so we could find seats together. We even managed to find a window seat. Later, on our approach to Pakistan, I looked out the window, shocked. One of the engines was on fire! The guy in the seat in front of me looked back at me, wide-eyed. I pressed my finger to my lips, asking him to keep quiet about it. I then enlisted the people behind me not to let the rest of the passengers become aware of the burning engine. Our row seemed to cotton on, as none of us wanted any panic.

Judging by the crew's frantic actions back and forth from the cockpit, it was obvious that we didn't have to tell them about the burning engine. We did try; however, they just brushed past as if they hadn't heard us. The seat belt sign had come on, and then without any explanation, the Captain announced that we would be stopping over in Karachi in Pakistan. We could clearly hear the quiver in his voice.

I watched as the plane banked, leveled out over the ocean, and dumped its fuel. We landed on the Karachi runway with fire engines speeding down both sides of the plane - thankfully, they were not needed. I reckon more than half the passengers on the plane never knew what had just happened.

We had to wait for a replacement airplane at the Karachi airport for twenty-two hours. You get what you pay for, they say. I am glad, though, that we did not have to pay the ultimate price. The backup plane arrived, and we finally found ourselves on our way to Sri Lanka.

At night, we arrived in the capital, Colombo. I often find that when I arrive at a new place in the dark, I experience the arrival twice, as come daylight it somehow seems like a different place. We cleared customs okay, hailed a banged-up old taxi, and made our way to the small fishing village of Negombo, an hour away on the west coast of Sri Lanka. It was hot and humid, and the taxi's small fan made more noise than wind. We drove past silhouettes of Hindi and Buddhist temples, and later large mosques, and then Catholic churches. It already reflected the rich diversity of cultures on this island.

Our friend and advisor Justin in Sri Lanka.
Note: His beat-up old taxi behind.

Once out of town, we saw the first coconut palm against the full moon, and then the golden beaches and open ocean. I was tired but couldn't help the excitement rising in me and wondering what the daylight would reveal. Our taxi driver introduced himself as Justin. He told us the old taxi belonged to him and that his home was close to where we were going. He then offered to be our guide and "adviser" on any matters while in his country. I admit that I was wary of his offer at first, but as it turned out, Justin, his wife, and four kids became wonderfully close friends. He turned out to be an absolute godsend, helping us out with several issues, always ready to drive us to wherever we wished to go.

Eventually, after many tips and dos and don'ts from Justin, we arrived at a seaside bungalow that we had rented in advance. The bungalow was right on the beach, with the moonlit sea bowing and retreating gently just a few meters away. Although we had arrived in the early hours of the morning, someone was there to meet us and show us our accommodation. By the time we had unpacked, the glow of the rising sun began to show behind the edge of the flat, calm sea.

Elisabeth and I went down to sit on the beach to watch the sunrise. It rose to reveal several fishing dhows, their sails in the wind, as they headed out to the horizon. It was a magical sight. Little was I to know, six months from now, we would attempt to be the first to cross that ocean in a forty-foot motorboat - perhaps ever.

The dhows in Sri Lanka return after a day's fishing,

GORDON S. BRACE

Our six months in Sri Lanka is a story in itself; however, I will leave most of that tale for another time. But here is some of it.

Justin later found a more permanent three-bedroom bungalow for us to rent, which was close to the beach and near a tourist hotel. The hotel became a hangout for us to meet people from around the world and network with some locals.

The newly built house had no furniture or utensils for cooking and washing. Justin said he knew of a place that had everything one needed for the house, from pots and pans, to furniture, to rice and fruit. In fact, there was little this massive warehouse shop didn't have.

Justin insisted on doing the shopping for us. His reasoning was that wherever one goes in Sri Lanka, there is one price for the locals and then a "tourist price" for visitors, with the price depending on one's accent. It is true, though. Sri Lankans do love to bargain. However, once you've developed a tan, they know you've been around for a while, and then you'll find that prices can be knocked down on average by 50 percent.

By now, we were well aware of this, so Elisabeth kindly declined Justin's offer to do the shopping. She said, now that we were living in Sri Lanka, she would need to learn to handle this herself.

But Justin would not hear of it and insisted sternly: "Memsahib, Justin must do the shopping!" Elisabeth, however,

14

was just as insistent. Then Justin became adamant. "No, Memsahib, Justin *must* do the shopping!"

"No," responded Elisabeth. "Thank you, Justin, but I will do the shopping!"

I stayed out of it.

When we arrived at the warehouse to do the shopping, Justin remained sulking in his car. Elisabeth and I went in and bought a variety of goods, foodstuffs, and furniture, half of which was to be set aside to be delivered. The foodstuffs, however, were placed in boxes to be brought to the car. The manager attended to us, and Elisabeth handled the bargaining, telling him not to charge us the "tourist price," as "we were not tourists." After a lot of haggling and pretending to walk away, she knocked the price down the usual 50 percent.

Satisfied, Elisabeth paid the bills and then, along with a few young men carrying the boxes behind her, she proudly walked to the car, where Justin was waiting. He stepped out of the car, snatched the receipts from Elisabeth's hands, barked something in Sinhalese to the lads, and before we could say anything, marched them back to the shop with the boxes. We watched him approach the manager, (or owner) and a major altercation ensued. After some time and a lot of shouting, Justin stormed back to us at the car. He had a pile of money in his hand, which he shoved into Elisabeth's hands, declaring angrily, "Next time, Justin does the shopping!"

I couldn't help but burst into laughter. Elisabeth looked at me sheepishly, but then couldn't help but smile herself.

I had another hustle incident later, which is relevant to the sequence of events to follow. We were invited to have a meal with a local lifeguard and his family. After a modest meal of rice and fish, he took us on a tour of the living quarters. We came to one room that had just a single bed, a bench, and a table. He then proceeded to tell me that his grandmother slept here. He pointed out that the roof above the bed had a hole in it, resulting in his grandmother getting wet when the monsoons came, and could I help him with some money to fix it? I knew I was being hustled and usually wouldn't stand for it, but then I thought, *what the hell*, and I parted with enough money to get it fixed.

Believe it or not, just over a month later, the same guy made another offer for a meal with his family. I decided not to remind him that we had already been once before. Instead, I took him up on his offer again, only to be taken on the same tour, to the same room and with the same story. Here, I accosted him quite aggressively, saying I had already been here before and had given him money to fix that hole.

At first, he looked at me in horror, then gave me a huge smile, patted me on the back, and burst out laughing. "Yes, yes, I remember you now. You know, when de Swedish people coming, I make much money from dat hole!"

My anger at being ripped off began to subside as the humor of it occurred to me. Even though he had been caught, his cavalier attitude seemed to suggest, at least in his mind, that this con was totally acceptable, and that instead of being embarrassed, he found the situation quite funny. Once I no longer had a target on my back, we both relaxed and talked to each other far more openly.

During our discussion, I mentioned that I, too, was a certified lifeguard, to which he asked if I would consider helping them at the hotel. A couple of busloads of German tourists were arriving soon and, apparently, every season they always had problems with them getting into trouble while bathing in the sea with several apparently drowning. (He told us they had sixteen tourists drown that season along the coast, fourteen of whom were Germans.) The hotel management was more than happy for me to help. This would later lead me to an opportunity.

The boat I was negotiating to buy. Note: The Mako shark.

However, I was here to find out about purchasing and working on a fishing boat. So, with Justin's help, we checked out the harbors, fishing villages, and even the fishing boat factories so as to find new or used boats.

After a while, I found a used boat which came with a seasoned crew and fully equipped fishing gear. With Justin by my side, I negotiated a deal. Elisabeth, however, felt uneasy about it. She couldn't quite explain why she felt this way; Elisabeth just said it didn't feel right, she also reckoned the crew looked unsavory and she did not fancy waiting on shore while I was out at sea with "that lot". Elisabeth very rarely had misgivings about our adventures. Women's intuition is not to be sneered at, as I am told. So, I stalled, which was fortunate, as we discovered later that the deal would have been a bad one. So, I still kept an eye out for another opportunity.

Not long after we passed up on the deal, we were relaxing on our patio, enjoying the view with some new friends, when a local lifeguard ran up to our house in a panic, screaming that a couple of Germans were drowning. The local lifeguards were quite small guys, and the Germans were not.

I ran with him to the beach and swam out beyond the breakers, where another lifeguard did his best to assist an overweight elderly lady, who was trying to climb on top of him in a panic while the husband screamed for help close by. I managed to subdue the lady, who was quite a handful, while the local guys managed to deal with the husband, who was smaller (but not by much).

As I headed toward the beach with her, a sleek twenty-six-foot motorboat, powered by a 200 horsepower Mercury engine, was speeding toward us. On board, a sunbaked man in his late forties shouted at me in an unmistakable Australian accent: "Ya need some help there, mate?"

I shouted back my thanks, but figured I had things under control. Nevertheless, he beached his boat and swam out from the shore to give us a hand. Once we had the couple settled on deck chairs at the hotel poolside, the Australian man introduced himself and offered to buy me a drink. This man owned two powerboats, which he operated from one of Ngombo's major hotel resorts a few miles down the coast, catering for the water sport requirements of the guests, such as deep-sea fishing, waterskiing, and snorkeling trips, with paragliding as the main attraction.

We became friendly, and when I told him why I was in Sri Lanka, he said that maybe I was the guy he was looking for. He wanted to leave Sri Lanka and return to Australia for personal reasons, so he needed someone to take over his water sports business. He would train me in all aspects (especially the parasailing operation, of which I had no experience), and if I found it suited me, he would make a deal for me to buy him out and take over the business. Here was the opportunity I was looking for.

The setup appeared good, and I began to work with him and quickly got the hang of it. Within a couple weeks, I figured I was ready to take over. However, some funds we were waiting on to wrap up the deal were a couple of months off, and Elisabeth and I wanted to explore more of the island.

Parasailing in Sri Lanka

One thing I had heard about before arriving in Sri Lanka was a tale of a primitive people found in a remote part of the island. This isolated small tribe of the Vedda, I was told, were the Aboriginal people of Sri Lanka, dating back to the Stone Age. These were true wild people, still living as hunters and gatherers, their only clothing being loincloths, and some only wearing tree bark for covering. They still hunted with bow and arrow and poison plants. For many years, they had hidden away from modern civilizations that arrived in Sri Lanka and maintained their way of life by hiding in the jungle. Their own language is apparently something of a mystery and cannot be traced to any other language. Unfortunately, most of the Vedda tribe have recently been assimilated into modern society to the point where even their unique language is all but lost and their status is considered low. However, I was told that a small group had been discovered in a remote jungle close to the coast who still, by all accounts, lived as wild people, maintaining their ancient language and way of life untouched by the modern world.

I had met similar wild people of the bushman tribe of the Kalahari and had great respect and admiration for their amazing connection to nature. I wondered if these people might be of the same ilk, and if there was some way we could find and visit with them.

We had become friendly with a wealthy local man and his family. On mentioning the tribe to him, he was surprised that he had never heard of them. However, if we could substantiate there was something to it, he and a few family members would like to join us. He even offered to fund the expedition.

At first our inquiries were fruitless until I happened to mention it to Justin, who said that he had heard people talk of them, and even heard more or less where they lived. He reckoned if we went to that area, the people there should be able to direct us.

So, it was decided we would go and find out. It took us a full day of driving to finally reach the area. On arrival, we asked around and put the word out, though it seemed, even here, no one seemed to know who, or where, this primitive Vedda tribe was. We began to think that maybe the story of these people was just a myth.

Just as we decided to call it and return to Ngombo, an elderly man approached us and spoke in Sinhalese to my local friend. Our host turned to me, grinning, and said this man would take us there!

We found a place to stay for the night, and early the next day met up with our guide. It was quite an ordeal to get there through the jungle to the coast, but fortunately, we were in two 4x4 Land Rovers. We eventually broke through the jungle, arriving at the coast to a settlement of small huts close to the beach. It wasn't long before our presence was realized and announced. With great commotion, we were quickly surrounded by curious faces. Our guide told us that there had only ever been six white people here before us, so apparently, we were quite a novelty. As we got out of the vehicle, some of the tribe ran up to us and rubbed our skin, perhaps to see if the white would come off, then laughed and stepped back. They were fascinated by Elisabeth's hair.

The first thing that struck us was the atrocious smell. There were rotting green turtle carcasses all over the place, along with the remains of various fish. The next thing we noticed was the swarm of flies. It was only when we got down to the beach that we could get some respite from them. On our arrival, it became obvious that the modern world had arrived to some degree. No traditional clothing like I had expected, but everyone in the tribe was wearing Adidas shorts (even the women).

Arriving at the Vedda village.

We found it difficult to connect with the Vedda people. It was different from the bushman with whom I had interacted. I don't think it was just the language issue; there seemed to be an element of chaos. From the little I knew of these people, I gathered that, although they had lived primitively for centuries, they still had order and strong traditions, with strong tribal ties. There was little evidence of that here. It appeared to me the introduction to the modern world had stripped it away. Perhaps they still needed time to adjust.

We made our way down the seaside, where a lot of the smaller tropical coral fish lay discarded on the beach. The coral reefs in Ngombo were not the best I had seen, so I hoped that, perhaps, this indicated there was a relatively untouched coral reef close by.

A Vedda man, who looked like he would be at home on a pirate ship, was scaling a fish on the beach. So, I picked up a few of the tropical fish and walked up to him. I tried to ask him, using gestures, where I could go dive to find these fish. He looked up at me for a moment. Then, without warning, he raised the machete he was using and slashed it into the sand - an inch from my foot! - and then, with an almost toothless grimace, glared at me menacingly. I decided not to show fear and stared back at him. He then burst out laughing and walked away. I wondered what I had done to offend him. However, he walked over to a boat and nodded at me, then pointed out to sea and then back to the boat. Did he understand and was inviting me? I gestured to him just to wait and ran back to the Land Rover to get my diving gear, calling the rest of the crowd to join me and my toothless, mischievous "pirate."

We boarded his boat, and he took us to the best diving spot I've ever seen in Sri Lanka. There was a point on this dive when I had a somewhat scary moment. There is not much on a coral reef that scares me, but on this dive on this reef, a massive green head armed with several rows of vicious teeth shot out of a hole straight toward me and gaped at me just a few feet from my face. This was, and still is, the most massive moray eel I've ever seen. I will admit, his size and attitude had me backing out of there in great haste! I reckon he was at least six feet long with a head so big I figured he could easily swallow mine.

We left the Vedda people, waving a friendly goodbye. However, we had to travel for some time with all the doors open to get rid of the hordes of flies that had settled in the vehicles.

On our return to Ngombo, I completed my training with the parasailing and began to run the water sports business. Things were going well when a meeting was called by the Australian to discuss our takeover. During the meeting, a local man in a suit strutted over to our table, sat down, lounged back in his chair, and looked at me arrogantly. Without introducing himself, he declared, "In my business, you will not use these boats to run drugs from India!"

I have little time for ill-mannered people, and my anger immediately rose at his attitude. So, I ignored him and said to the Australian, "Who the hell is this guy, and who is he to even insinuate I would be a drug smuggler?"

The local guy sat forward as if to intimidate me and said, "I will be the senior partner in this business."

I leaned forward, myself, within an inch from his face and looked him in the eye. "The hell you will!" I retorted, leaving him with no doubt on that fact.

When I offered to purchase his business, the Australian had assured me that because he had been invited by the government to set up the water sport business, the usual 51 percent that would usually go to a local had been waived, and he could maintain 100 percent ownership.

"Hang on, hang on," said the Aussie. "Gordon, I know this guy, and because you're buying the business here, he will be the 51 percent local 'partner.'"

I immediately smelled a rat. This was too new and sudden. "So, where is his 51 percent contribution to the costs?" I asked.

"It doesn't work like that," he responded. "You still have to pay the full amount."

I went on to say, "That was not the deal, and if it was, I could go into the street and invite any local to be that partner before this ill-mannered, arrogant man who happens to be your friend! If you guys think you can intimidate me into agreeing to this, you don't know who you're dealing with!" I got up and walked away, ignoring their pleas to come back.

The following day, Elisabeth and I went to the hotel, where the Australian and his local friend were waiting for me. They approached and asked if we could talk. I said I would, but not to his so-called partner. So, the Australian and I had a one-on-one. The more he spoke, the less I trusted him.

During our chat, he mentioned there was another guy from Kenya who operated a game fishing operation at Trincomalee, and if I spoke to him, he would corroborate his story regarding partnership requirements in Sri Lanka. When I asked who he was, he responded with the name Ken Oulton. To my surprise, this was a name I knew well! In fact, Ken was well known throughout Kenya for many reasons - some good, some not so good. He was known as a top rugby player, an East African rally driver, a mercenary, and one of the top big-game fishermen, claiming some world records. He was a larger-than-life character. Another reason I knew of him was that he was a close neighbor of my family when they farmed in Kenya.

Needless to say, a few days later, we found ourselves headed for Trincomalee on the other side of the island. This was quite a trip where rules of the road didn't seem to apply, and several elephants had to be negotiated. We had been told Ken's game fishing boat was moored at the main harbor, so Elisabeth and I made our way there. However, on arrival at the entrance, we were denied entry to the harbor. That is, until we mentioned Ken's name, upon which the boom was raised immediately. (It seemed Ken's reputation had followed him here.) At the moorings, we spotted a sleek forty-foot wooden game fishing vessel. On our approach, we saw two men working in earnest on the boat.

The man who first caught my attention stood a good six-foot-seven inches tall. He was tanned a leathery brown from constant exposure to the tropical sun. Though he was so tall, he carried himself well, and what he carried was a powerful, wiry frame without an ounce of fat showing. Without being told, one would never have guessed he was in his early fifties. This was Ken Oulton, the skipper, owner of the sport fishing boat—the good ship, *Miken*. Perhaps one day this man may tell his own story, as it is surely a story worth the pen.

I hailed permission to board. Ken welcomed us aboard and introduced us to the young New Zealander working with him, David Faulkner. Dave, who was in his early twenties, had a crop of curly fair hair with one of those pleasant faces you can't help but immediately like. He was a good six feet tall himself. A confirmed surfing fanatic, he spent his time chasing the best waves around the world, and like most surfers I knew, he looked strong and well built.

As Ken was twice my age, he said he didn't remember me from Kenya (a different generation) except for a story of when I was a young boy visiting there.

Back then, any person who arrived at my uncle's farm was always warned to stay away from his prize bull. It was renowned as a "killer bull" and would attack anybody without hesitation. I had gone missing soon after arriving on the farm, and the family immediately figured I, of course, had gone to see the bull. They all rushed down to the bullpen, my uncle's rifle in hand, to find me stroking the big animal, saying he was not a bad bull at all! My uncle, rifle at the ready, coaxed me to the railing, with the bull walking meekly behind me. Without having to shoot his prize bull, he managed to pull me out of the pen. Instead of giving me a hiding, he apparently shed a few tears. Ken said that was a well-known story of the day, so he was glad to meet that boy now as a man, and of course, he did remember that event and had known my family very well. There was an obvious air of preparation about the boat, so I asked Ken if he was planning a trip. Here he dropped a bombshell.

Yes, he was planning a trip. He was planning to take his forty-foot game fishing boat, the *Miken*, approximately four thousand nautical miles across the Indian Ocean to Kenya!

To his knowledge, this had never before been attempted across this ocean in a single-engine motorboat.

Many motorboats had attempted crossing the Atlantic, as there, they were surrounded by first-world countries with good support systems. Any of the many ships in that ocean would come to a boat's assistance should the need arise. However, the Indian Ocean was different, as this was third world, with little to no support systems for search and rescue. Another factor was piracy. Ships that had previously assisted boats that appeared in distress found that these boats were actually pirate traps, as armed men waited below decks to take over the ship. These were also the days of the "boat people" refugees. Apparently, if a ship or tanker stopped to help them, the rescuers had to take the refugees all the way back to the ship's port of registration, not the next port of call, which resulted in them not offering assistance at all. So, no brotherhood at sea in this ocean.

Until now, there had not been any attempts to cross these seas in a motorboat for several reasons. So, if one did, you could expect to be entirely on your own, and should anything go wrong, one would be unlikely to get help from any quarter. (We would experience this firsthand.) So, this attempt would be the first.

Ken went on to say he would cross from Sri Lanka to the Maldives, then to the uninhabited islands of the Great Chagos Bank right in the middle of the Indian Ocean, well over a thousand miles from the nearest civilization. Once there, he hoped to dive for shells to help pay for the trip, but most importantly, there was another reason - and, in fact, the most important reason - to head for those islands that would even allow this attempt.

Ken had started hatching his plan after he met some people who were circumnavigating the globe by yacht. On their way to Sri Lanka, they had chanced upon the Peros Banhos Atoll in the Chagos Bank, when they were actually looking for the Salomon Atoll, as the latter was known for its good anchorage, whereas Peros was not. However, as they were there, they decided to explore the largest of the twenty-nine islands in the atoll. They told Ken there must have been an expedition there in the distant past, as in the jungle they stumbled upon a large stack of stainless-steel drums of diesel fuel. They couldn't say how much was there, as most of the stack was covered by jungle vine. A few drums seemed empty, but others were definitely full. Without that information, this expedition would not be possible. That fuel would make it possible to cross the next thousand-mile leg to the Seychelles islands.

I knew right then this was what we were here for!

As it happens, one of Elisabeth's major interests was, and still is, shell collecting. Diving for shells was nothing new to me, as I had professionally done just that in several places around the world, especially in the Caribbean.

While living and diving there with the locals, I had also learned a lot from my island friends about how to survive on a tropical island. Even while here in Sri Lanka, I had picked up tips in that regard, as it was something of interest to me. My survival skills growing up in the African Bush might also come in handy, and having some knowledge of motorboats, fishing, spearfishing, and diving all seemed to have been an apprenticeship for this adventure.

I mentioned this to Ken and asked him if he might have room for two more people.

Ken said, "Great, you're just who I'm looking for myself!"

He invited us back to his house, where we discussed the planned venture in detail. Pointing out the obvious dangers of crossing four thousand nautical miles open sea in a single-engine motorboat, which, unlike a sailboat, has no keel, but has a shallow draft and only one inboard motor to rely on.

Because of the risks involved in a venture like this, Ken asked us not to make an immediate decision but to go away and think on it for a while, then get back to him.

Elisabeth and I went down the coast and found a quiet spot. We sat at the water's edge with our feet in the sea, looking out at that big ocean.

Elisabeth turned to me and said, "So, what do you think?"

"I think you know what I think," I responded.

She looked at me and said, "I know you often feel invincible and will take on most things, and I have come to trust in that, so if you feel we can do this, let's do it!"

I reminded her of the maxim, "You should rather die regretting the things you have done than regretting things you haven't done." (Although, I do have a proviso that it should not be at anyone else's expense. In this case, I had to consider whether the expense would be the ultimate price.) This would put Elisabeth into an extremely risky venture, albeit a calculated risk.

It is difficult to explain this, and may seem fanciful, but since I was a young boy, I have always felt there was a guardian angel watching over me, and Elisabeth now that she was in my life. So, I truly did believe that the adventure presented to us was not by chance, and that we would survive it no matter what.

An hour later, we found ourselves driving back to Ken. We would be coming!

Shortly after that, we were sitting once again with Dave and Ken, planning to be the first people to cross the Indian Ocean in a motorboat. Along the way, we would visit tropical islands and coral reefs to dive and game fish.

Ken suggested we sort out our affairs back in Ngombo as soon as we can and return to help prepare for the journey. We could stay in his bungalow and assist with getting the boat ready. Ken said he still had some customers coming in for a couple of deep-sea fishing trips, which he would like to wrap up before we left. Ken had told us his business wasn't doing so well here in Sri Lanka. Later on, I was to find out one of the reasons why. Elisabeth and I returned to our home in Ngombo and settled our affairs. One evening, someone knocked at our door. I was not very surprised to see it was the Australian coming to talk to me about his water sports business. However, accompanying him was a local gentleman whom I did not know, dressed in a suit. We invited them in.

The stranger turned out to be a minister from the ministry of tourism. He introduced himself and immediately told me why he was there. He had been told that I walked out of the deal, and why, and he was there to assure me that if I bought the water sports business from the Australian, I wouldn't need a partner but could take over at the original agreement of 100 percent ownership. I looked over at Elisabeth. *What now?*

I thanked him and said I would consider it, but that another opportunity had presented itself. He asked what it was. After I told him, both he and the Australian reacted, "Are you crazy!" The Australian added a few expletives.

Well, I guess sometimes it helps to be more than a little crazy, for a few days later, after a final meal with Justin and his family, and a sad farewell after attending a colorful and moving communion ceremony for his children.

Justins son and daughter's confirmation ceremony in Sri Lanka

We headed for Trincomalee to prepare for a once-in-a-lifetime epic journey. There was no way we were going to miss out on an adventure like that! We wouldn't die one day wondering, "What if?"

Preparing the Miken

We settled into Ken's home and immediately began to discuss what still needed to be done on the *Miken* and what supplies we would need.

However, Ken said he had five German customers arriving the following day to go fishing for billfish, either sailfin or marlin. He asked if I would join him. It was on this fishing trip that I was to get a first taste of Ken's reputation.

At sunrise the next day, we were headed out to the blue water. The fishing rods were laid out, two on the booms and one in front of the fighting chair. It then occurred to one of the clients that there was only one fighting chair, but five people. It wasn't long before they were arguing about who was going to be first. Before I could suggest drawing matchsticks, one of them insisted he was going first, went to the fighting chair, sat down, and claimed it. After an hour of trawling with no action on the rods, Ken and I noticed that the guy in the fighting chair had fallen asleep; Ken reacted angrily.

"Is that asshole who made all that noise about being first now sleeping in my fighting chair!" he barked. He slid down from the flybridge to the lower deck, approached the other four clients, and told them, in no uncertain terms, they were *not* to say anything! Then he pulled in one of the lines, attached a plastic bucket to the end, and dropped it overboard.

The rod screamed in agony, instantly waking the client in the fighting chair. He grabbed the rod, eyes full of excitement, and began to fight the bucket. Ken even opened the throttle a couple of times to make it more difficult for him.

After watching him suffer for a good ten minutes, Ken ended his pain and unrequited expectation of a monster game fish, then walked up to him and stated as matter of fact, "Okay, you've had your turn." He then grabbed one of the other clients, shoved him toward the fighting chair, and informed him, "You're next!"

A few days later, another group of German clients arrived, specifically for mako shark, the only shark considered a game fish. We collected a drum of chum and blood for a scent trail, and once again headed for the deep blue. I have personally seen the nearby fishing harbor lined up with mako shark from one end of the pier to the other. However, this does not mean that one will find these game sharks on every trip.

After the first chum trail, we had no luck, so we upped lines and went to another area, where we laid out chum behind the boat again. As we finished laying the scent trail, one of the clients turned to his friends and, making certain we could obviously hear him, said clearly in plain English, "This is a waste of time and a f—ing rip-off. There are no sharks here!"

Ken bounded from the helm and down the flybridge ladder in an instant, grabbed the man by the seat of his pants, and ran him off the low transom astern, and into the sea. It didn't take the man long to realize he was treading water in chum laid out for sharks, and he started to scream at us to get him out. Ken casually waved him off and said, "Cool off, mate, don't worry about it. You just said yourself, there are no f—ing sharks here." Then he strolled off to the flybridge, leaving me and his friends to get the terrified man out of the water.

As most of Ken's clients were, for the most part, Germans, this gave me an insight as to perhaps why Ken's game fishing business was not doing so well here in Sri Lanka. As amusing as I found the incidents, it also gave me some insight into the man himself.

That was Ken's last booking, so now we completely devoted our time to prepare for the journey to cross the Indian Ocean. Ken already had a preliminary list of supplies, and Elisabeth and I made a few more suggestions.

As the bulk of what we could carry had to be drinking water and fuel, weight and space was a factor. So, Elisabeth worked out a daily menu of basic foodstuffs, keeping in mind we should be able to catch fish and dive the islands for seafood along the way.

Getting the Miken ready for her epic journey.

For those who may be interested, the main bulk of our weight was obviously fuel in long-range fuel tanks, forty-five-gallon drums strapped to the deck, and water tanks. Other supplies consisted of flour, rice, sugar, canned meat and fruit, tea, coffee, powered milk, kerosene, fruit drinks, five gallons of arrack (an alcohol of coconut palm extract), some rum, oats, biscuits, glucose sweets and fresh fruit, a few boxes of macaroni, some jams, gardening tools and a machete (which Ken already owned), usual cutlery, crockery, pots and pans, a very useful Chinese wok, an iron wood fire stove, and kerosene lamps. We each allowed ourselves one or two small luxuries. Mine was a good bottle of brandy in anticipation of some great sundowners.

Ken was friendly with a local doctor and managed to obtain from him certain essentials for a medical kit, such as morphine and, very important, serum for the poison of stonefish. The rest was made up of the usual bandages, ointments, and antibiotics.

Each day we returned home from working on the boat, Ken anxiously checked his incoming mail. A few days before we were due to leave, he received the telegram he had been waiting for. We were to be joined by a fifth member.

Nicole Hascoet arrived from France a couple of days later. Nicole turned out to be a pleasant, dark-haired lady in her mid-thirties, very relaxed, easygoing, and full of charm. She wasted no time in joining in the spirit of the venture and got stuck in helping us load the supplies. Some painting and antifouling needed doing, so the two girls got to know each other by getting stuck into that job together.

Nicole loading supplies from Kens' bungalow in Sri Lanka.

Dave was also waiting on his girlfriend in New Zealand to join us, but for some reason, she could not make it. This concerned me a bit. There are books written about the dynamics of people put in relatively close spaces for any length of time (especially long sailing trips), the possible disputes and conflicts that could arise, the different permeations involved, what to be aware of, what pitfalls to avoid, and how to deal with certain situations. One of the main pieces of advice I've heard is, if possible, try not to leave someone in the group as an odd one out - in this case, two couples and one loner. Dave said it wouldn't bother him, and as we were getting on so well together, I put it out of my mind.

Ken dismantled his bed and loaded it. We also loaded his cane chairs and tables, which were tied down to the deck of the flybridge. There were to be many occasions in the days to come when we would be grateful for them. We also loaded a cane basket for a pet mongoose I had acquired named Paradise. Paradise was an extremely tame bundle of energy and mischief; he was to give us many hours of company and amusement.

We discussed one of the main concerns of our expedition, which was, of course, our total reliance on a single-diesel-engine motorboat. (We did have an auxiliary twenty-five horsepower outboard engine on board, and a small amount of petrol. However, other than perhaps using it to navigate the islands, it had limited application.) Ken's plan was to mount a mast in the forecastle of the *Miken* so as to rig a square sail for backup. As the *Miken* had no keel and drew only four feet of water, this could only work if we had a following wind. We would then, more than likely, have to cut and dump the high flybridge. It wasn't much of a backup, but was something at least, so we set it up.

Ken had planned this journey for December, as it should have been the end of the Sri Lankan and Maldivian cyclone (monsoon) storm season, and so the seas should have been relatively calmer. Little did we know what was waiting for us.

The transom of the *Miken* was fairly low to the waterline, which is helpful when catching big gamefish. But I was not happy with it like that, as I was concerned in the open ocean, in rough seas we would take a lot of water astern. Ken agreed and suggested

Dave and I come up with a plan. So, we went into town and bought a plank that was long and high enough to extend the transom. It was the last thing that needed doing.

When Dave and I had securely fixed the plank, Ken nodded with approval. "We're going to bless that thing," he said. At that moment, he didn't know how right he would be, though not only for the job it was intended for. It was the last thing that needed doing - we were ready to go...

Getting to Know You

The *"Miken"* journal reads simply:

December 1980 the 8th.
Left Trincomalee harbor 12.38 hours.
Nicole made a lovely cup of tea with cake.
"Paradise" has quietened down

The first leg of the journey would take us approximately three hundred miles along the east coast of Sri Lanka to the port of Galle on the southern tip of the island.

This journey would give us the chance to see how we worked together in a confined space, to get to know the boat, and to discover any items needed for our trip that we may have overlooked. Galle would be our last chance to rectify any oversight or to revoke any decision. Once we parted from Galle, it would be our Rubicon - there would be no turning back. And we would be completely alone in that massive expanse of the Indian Ocean.

For this part of the journey, Ken, Dave, and I rotated three hourly shifts at the helm while Nicole and Elisabeth organized our meals, kept us company, and regularly brought us a welcomed mug of hot tea or coffee.

Paradise keeping Gordon company at the helm.

The *Miken* rode the waves well, her 175-horsepower purred maternally; a continuous, gentle, reassuring sound. Ken had designed and built the boat in the company of a friend of his named Mike - thus *"Miken."* They specifically built her as a big-game fishing boat. This was Ken's profession, and his boat boasted a splendid collection of big-game fishing equipment.

Elisabeth scanning the horizon.

The thrill of big-game fishing is something I have a passion for, so when I was not on shift, I spent a great deal of my time in the fighting chair, waiting for that telltale scream of the ratchet as a big fish runs with line. I did not have long to wait. Soon out from Trincomalee, I landed my first fish, a small member of the tuna family, a bonito. This is a good eating fish, and one that was to become a regular part of our diet. I landed a couple more, as they are also good bait for marlin.

We had our first trouble shortly after this fish was caught: our steering failed. We drifted a while as we searched for the problem, and we discovered the steering cable had come loose. We repaired it the best we could and continued on our way. Not long afterward, the steering failed again.

This was the second stop of many that we would have to make; that cable plagued us right through the night. At one time we drifted, or I should say rocked and rolled, for three hours in uncomfortable seas to work on the problem. In the dark seas about us, the waves crashed louder and louder, each passing minute bringing us ever closer to the patient teeth of the offshore reef. Ken shouted for me to get the square-rig sail canvas and fashion a drogue with it to make a parachute type sea anchor to drag behind the boat so as to slow us down. Fortunately, it was not needed, as Ken made repairs timeously and cheated the reef with only a few yards to spare.

This was too close for comfort, so we decided to head a fair distance away from the coastline.

Later, Ken was at the helm, and I was below on deck when I thought I heard someone shouting. I dismissed it at first, but then I heard it again, and this time louder. I ran to the bow and looked out into the dark seas. There was nothing to see, but I now distinctly heard a person screaming frantically. In the dark, someone was desperately trying to light a lantern, and I could vaguely make out people rowing like hell in a small boat that we were bearing down on!

I turned to Ken. "Come to port! Come to port!"

Ken did not hesitate - another close call, as we barely missed running the smaller boat down. However, we discovered this was not to be the only boat out in the dark sea. Fishing boats and dhows were everywhere, none of which had the required navigation lights (except when, on seeing us, some of them lit up lanterns and waved them at us). So, through the night, we had to take shifts sitting on the bow and peering into the dark, so as to warn whoever was on shift at the helm. Even then, there were other, even more close shaves that accompanied a lot of expletives from both the fishermen and us!

When the morning dawned on calm seas, we were pretty tired, so we decided to take turns sleeping. It also gave us a chance to properly fix the steering cable.

Extract from journal:

1980 December 9th.
Caught a seer fish. 8.13. Little Basque lighthouse.
Compass reading between the two Basque lighthouses
　　First reading 225
　　Second reading 230
We saw a whale off Great Basque lighthouse. 13.15. off
Hambantota, off the southern point. Had a light shower
of rain.
Arrived Galle Harbour 2100 hours. We made some fish
and chips and all had some much needed sleep.

On our first morning in Galle, we met a few "yachties" in the harbor, who were passing through on their around-the-world travels, and we swapped banter with them. These were the days when yachtsmen sailing around the world were few, so they were a close-knit bunch. When it came to sailing, were pretty much (what I call) purists. So, when they found out we planned to cross the ocean in a forty-foot motorboat, we received no end of flack from them regarding our venture.

One English skipper constantly scoffed at us. "Cross the ocean in that bathtub? You must be bloody barmy!"

"Of course we are, you snotty yachtie," I retorted. "He who dares!"

He laughed and later invited us to join him and other yachtsmen on shore for dinner that night at "Don's place."

Don Windsor was a well-to-do local businessman who had a soft spot for the visiting sailors, and kindly opened his doors and offered his advice and amenities to any yachties who called in at Galle Harbor. We all had a hot shower at his place. After we were cleaned up, we joined the other yachtsmen, where Don had a wonderful meal prepared for all of us.

Before the meal, though, Don brought some sad news, after which we all stood for a minute's silence in remembrance of two families who had recently had a tragedy at sea. I do not suffer nightmares, but this story did linger in my mind for quite a while. Don told us that his and a few of the yachtie's friends, two Scandinavian families, were circumnavigating on a schooner, and had recently left Sri Lanka, headed for Madagascar. On the way, they found themselves becalmed in the scorching heat of Doldrums. They all jumped overboard for a swim to cool off. Once in the water, however, they were horrified to find they had broken a golden rule: no one had dropped the boarding ladder or stayed on board. One would think there must be a way to get back on board, but these were seasoned sailors, and no matter how hard they tried, they could not find a way. All except one were lost, drowned at sea. One of the fathers, miraculously picked up by a fishing trawler, was apparently still holding his youngest daughter, dead in his arms. It was a sobering story and reminded us the sea does take lives.

We stayed for five days in Galle, as some of us had some unfinished business to attend to in Colombo and elsewhere. Here we also purchased any outstanding supplies, refueled, and restocked with fresh fruit and coconuts.

We even acquired five chickens. Dave and I asked a local gentleman (who could not speak English) if he could acquire for us one male chicken and four lady chickens. This had us clucking and crowing while flapping our arms and gesturing with one finger in as deep a voice we could muster, the finger gesture denoting both amount and gender. Then in our most high-pitched tone, we strutted and swayed our butts as ladylike as we could— four of those! We also asked him if he could find some rabbits for us as well. This produced a great deal of hopping about on our part as well, even an "Eh, what's up Doc!"

The man, though highly amused by our antics, had absolutely no inkling of that requirement. He did, however, arrive later with four half-grown chicks and a magnificent cockerel, who we, of course, named "Cocky." On our last evening in Galle, we made ourselves comfortable in the cane chairs on the flybridge, found some soft music on our radio, and relaxed with a mug of arrack. The small harbor of Galle was quiet and peaceful. Various national flags fluttered in a gentle breeze on the yachts that rested about us, their different forms shaping their own peculiar silhouettes against a golden sky reflecting on a golden sea. We were ready to go.

Open Sea and the Maldives Islands

At 5:00 a.m. on Sunday, December 14, 1980, we set our course for the Maldives Islands, the only land for over a thousand nautical miles. We hauled up anchor, turned the bow of the *Miken* away from land, and headed out into that big, open ocean.

The sun rose spectacularly, turning the calm sea a golden hue, disturbed only by the *Miken* and a pod of dolphins on the bow leading us away. I sat with Elisabeth on the foredeck, none of us saying a word in fear of breaking the spell. As Sri Lanka disappeared behind us, I do remember feeling vulnerable and small - very, very small - but, strangely, more excited than apprehensive. The first day passed peacefully without event.

The following day, a fair breeze gave us the opportunity to try out our square-rig sail. The result was a slow two knots, and that only with a following wind, but at least it was something.

51

Early that afternoon, we had our first marlin-strike. Pandemonium broke loose on the boat as the excitement of the fight gripped all of us. It was short-lived; the magnificent fish came clear out of the water, shook its head, and threw the lure. We did not suffer the disappointment long, though. That afternoon, our patience was rewarded with three more strikes. Ken is a member of the IGFA, (International Game fishing Association) and so can claim world records. If he reckoned any of the billfish were close to a record, we would have landed them to weigh them, and although we did have some good-sized fish and some lengthy, exciting battles, none were in the record class, so after a good fight, we gave slack or removed the hook to let them go.

However, our excitement of fighting a big fish was tempered by Ken, who would scream in our faces every time we hooked a big fish, bark orders at the ladies to reel in the other lines, and swear at whoever was either in the fighting chair or guiding it, usually Dave or myself. As it was easier to get records for women, Ken tried to get the ladies to fish. However, because of his apparent insanity every time we hooked a big fish, they became too afraid to even try. After a few hits, even Dave declined to fish any longer and just guided the chair.

A couple of evenings later, we all went up to the flybridge to enjoy a ration of rum for a sundowner. Ken looked around at us and obviously realized he had an unhappy crew, so he apologized for his behavior, then asked us not to take it seriously because he just gets overexcited.

The following day, we had a marlin-strike again. The ladies ran to reel in the other lines; Dave was already behind the fighting chair. I was determined to enjoy this battle with the marlin, keeping in mind what Ken had said the previous evening (that is, to not take him seriously). I purposely took my time, and true to form, as though he could not help himself, Ken was screaming at me again, so loudly that I thought he might burst a blood vessel. I ignored him, strapped in, and hit the line. In the distance, a fair-sized marlin broke the surface, at which Ken bent over, screaming in my ear.

I stopped fishing and turned to him. "Ken!"

"What!" he retorted.

"F—k off!" I shouted back in his face.

Ken stared at me. I don't often swear, but it seemed to have the desired effect, for the six-foot-seven mercenary turned around, strode up to the flybridge, and seemed to sulk there for some time. After that, we all enjoyed the fishing, and Ken never screamed at us again.

At 5:30 a.m. on the morning of Tuesday, December 16, a great whoop awoke us as Ken cried, "Land Ho!"

And, indeed, there before us, through the mist of the early dawn, we vaguely made out the outline of an atoll, and distinctly heard the crashing of seas pounding against coral reef.

As the sun rose and the early-morning mist cleared, something out of a Disney motion picture unfolded before us like some fantasy. The deep, blue sea spent its energy on the ocean side of the reef. Beyond the reef on a coral table, the sea rested in tranquil emerald-green waters, which eventually lapped gently against white beaches fringed by tall, swaying palm trees. There were a few islands in this atoll, none of them more than a mile long. This was in the days before the Maldives became a tourist mecca with resorts everywhere. Tourists were rare, and most of the islands were uninhabited.

According to our calculations, we should have been at an atoll named Suvadiva, but the islands before us did not correspond to those on our charts. However, we all decided, before anything else, to find an anchorage and go ashore. The charts could be studied in more detail later. While we searched for a suitable spot, we caught a few fish from the reef to take with us ashore and cook them there for a picnic lunch on one of the beaches. Eventually, we sighted an enchanting little cove on the leeward side of one of the small islands.

An enchanting cove, our first stop in the Maldives.

Dave and I wasted little time. Before the *Miken* had even swung around on her anchor, we had donned our diving gear and dove into the crystal-clear water.

The sight that met our eyes below the water was breathtaking (which was helpful, as we were diving). There were magnificent coral formations, some heavy and masculine, sculptures of strange mythical gods. Others that were soft, feminine, and brightly colored gently swayed to-and-fro in a Garden of Eden. About the corals, many different species of tropical fish swam in abundance, a display in evidence of the magical artistry of Mother Nature. The odd reef shark, turtle, or ray passed by, paying us no mind.

After the dive, Dave and I explored part of the islands for a while and then rejoined the others, who had rowed ashore in the dinghy and were now relaxing on the beach in the shade of coconut palms.

If we spoke at all, we did softly, as it was a "don't wake me, I'm having a wonderful dream" situation. We just rested on the beach, enjoying the moment, when suddenly and very strangely, a weather-creased old man and a small dark boy materialized out of the foliage. They were, as far as we could ascertain, alone on this island. There was a language barrier, so we could not find out or make sense of their presence here.

I offered the old man some cigarettes, which he accepted gratefully, then carefully counted them out and gave exactly half to the small boy, which again did not make sense to me. Using gestures, they asked me to follow them. They led me to a place where a short, green plant was growing like a weed. The old man rubbed his tummy and made bubbling noises to indicate that this plant boiled and would be very good to eat. Then they proceeded to pick as much as I could carry, and with my hands full, I returned to the others. Ken said he knew the plant and that it was edible, so for our picnic we had barracuda, rice, and weed (or wild spinach).

Three o'clock that afternoon, we bid a farewell to the old man, the small boy, and their beautiful little island, perplexed as to why they were there alone, perhaps for some ritual. We never did find an explanation.

Our earlier suspicion became apparent as we sailed farther south: we had not arrived at the Suvadiva Atoll. After close scrutiny of the charts, we discovered we were still a good ninety miles north of there. The only explanation we could find for this significant error was that our compass might be reading incorrectly. If this was so, then we had been very lucky not to have missed the Maldives completely. We could not afford a mistake like this, because unlike a yacht, we had fuel consumption to consider.

In the late hours of the afternoon, the sea turned angry; storm weather was obviously approaching. As if sent to try us, the bilge pump packed up. We did not relish the idea of bailing with buckets in a storm, so we decided to seek shelter inside one of the atolls for the night. This was easier said than done. The reef stretched for miles, and the charts showed no gap.

We were about to resign ourselves to ride out the storm when, in the distance, we sighted a small, local fishing craft pass through the reef. There had to be a gap there! We kept our eyes glued to the spot. On our approach, we noticed some dolphins clearing the waves, as if to show us the way. The daylight held just long enough for us to find the passage. We followed the dolphins and joined the Maldivian fishing boat in the shelter of the leeward side of an island, where we stayed the night.

By the morning, the fury of the storm had passed. The sea was still rough, but we had repaired the bilge pump, so we decided to press on. As we left the shelter of the atoll, our school of dolphins was there and escorted us back out to sea.

I put two fishing lines out. It wasn't long before the boom snapped back, and the reel screeched as the line peeled away. As I struck the rod, a sailfin billfish, known as one of the fastest fish in the sea, tail-walked behind the boat on the water's surface. Dave went for the other line to reel it in, when Ken shouted at him from the flybridge, "Leave it!"

As Dave turned inquiringly, another sailfin hit his rod— we had a double! We had great fun as we battled them for a while. Eventually, one came off, and we let the other go. They are good eating, but it was too much meat for us to keep, so it would have been a waste to land them. I landed a nice sized snapper for supper instead.

Snapper for Supper.

We sailed the rest of the day and into the night down the Maldives' string of islands (around 1,200 of them) and headed for its most southern tip.

Arriving in the Maldives.

That night, we had to be satisfied with tinned food for supper. The rough seas made it impossible for the ladies to cook the few fish we had caught during the day.

At one o'clock in the early morning, we spotted a ship's light in the dark. It was obviously anchored in the lagoon of an atoll. We searched to find an entrance into the lagoon for two hours, but the darkness made this impossible. Eventually, however, we found a place of shelter in shallow water between two islands alongside the atoll. Just across from us on the far side of the reef, a large ship lay in quiet waters, all lit up like a Christmas tree.

At sunrise on the morning of Thursday, December 18, we entered the lagoon and came alongside the *Pontevedra*, a large Spanish fish-factory ship from Gran Canaries, then tied up at her stern.

As we rowed in our dinghy, strong currents made it difficult for us to reach a rope ladder that had been dropped for us from the lower deck amidships. We managed to reach the ladder, however, and once on board, were received heartily by the Captain, a good-looking man in his early thirties with classic dark Mediterranean features. He introduced himself as Antonio.

In the company of four other Spaniards, we were treated to a sumptuous lunch, after which we relaxed to enjoy ice-cold beers. We discussed our error on navigation, so Antonio asked us to bring the *Miken* further up alongside the *Pontevedra* and tie her amidships below the rope ladder so he may compare our compass readings. When we had her alongside, I remember how ridiculously like a matchbox toy the *Miken* appeared beside the factory ship. It turned out our compass was ten degrees in fault. Once this had been established, Antonio suggested a pleasure trip to Tinadu, or Thinadhoo, the main island of the Huvadhoo Atoll in the southern Maldives. We readily agreed and soon found ourselves in the ship's launch, headed across the lagoon toward the island.

Frangipani flowers being presented to the ladies.
Note: Spanish Skipper Antonio with them.

Dozens of small, dark, curious faces crowded the jetty to greet us. There were smiles of welcome from all the people we passed as we walked through coral streets fringed by small, uniformed, white-washed houses. However, all were men or boys; there was not a woman or a girl to be seen. It is said that the Maldives is the only place in the world that is 100 percent Muslim and has strict Muslim protocols, so I guess that had something to do with it. We were told later that (although no offense was intended) our ladies were frowned upon due to what the inhabitants considered skimpy attire for women. We were struck by how immaculately clean the small village was. Everything was in its proper place, neat and tidy.

The whole effect, however, was marred by two important-looking officials, who approached us dressed in Western-style business suits. Without explanation, they ordered us to leave the island. So, sad and perplexed, we returned to the launch. At the jetty, a crowd of small boys awaited us, where they offered, almost apologetically, bunches of frangipani flowers to the ladies.

Frangipanis being handed to the two ladies.

A party was held for us on the *Pontevedra* that night, with Chivas Regal whiskey as the main course. After the party, Ken had a serious accident. On our return to the *Miken*, he had jumped from the rope ladder onto her deck. The anchor lay unseen there in the darkness, its rusty points facing upward. Ken, barefooted, landed heavily on one of those points. His foot, badly pierced, bled copiously, and obviously needed medical attention. Ken waved aside any suggestion of a delay to seek medical help, doctored his foot as best he could himself, put a plastic bag over it, and declared we would leave the following day as planned. The island officials, however, had other ideas.

The following morning, an order arrived that we were not allowed to leave the atoll or board the *Pontevedra*. Antonio promised he would contact the island chief to find out what was going on. On his return, he informed us the Chief would be paying us a visit the following morning.

Tied up astern to the Spanish fish-factory ship.

We had no fresh fish that night, so Dave made a lovely rice pudding, which was really pretty good. We passed the evening by playing Scrabble on deck.

We awoke in the morning to the sound of rain, a sound which spurred us into action, as fresh water needed to be collected. We caught the water in buckets and pots as it ran from the decks and sunshade canvas. When the water containers were full, we all had a wash in the refreshing downpour. By ten thirty, the rain had passed and there was still no sign of the atoll Chief. The engineer of the *Pontevedra* sent us some freshly baked bread, which was much appreciated.

At midday, I suddenly remembered that Cocky, the cockerel, was still in a tin can, in which we had placed him during the rain shower and covered with a perforated plastic sheet. The temperature was well over 100°F. I tore at the cover to find, slumped in the bottom of the can, a half-steamed, filthy, brown bundle of feathers. I eased Cocky out of the can and placed him gently on my lap, his eyes closed while his head hung limp in my hand.

Ken took one look at him and said, "He's done, toss him!"

However, I figured I would see what I could do for him. I opened his beak slightly and poured a few drops of water down his throat. After a while, Cocky began to drink the water spasmodically on his own accord, and slowly, one of his eyes began to open. He gave me a "don't worry about me, fellows, save the women and children first" look. I assured him that we had the enemy on the run, then helped him to his feet and, with hands to support him, guided the cockerel around the deck. At first, he staggered drunkenly about, but shortly, I witnessed an amazing recovery. Within half an hour, Cocky was perched as proudly as ever on our turned-up dinghy, where, when he thought we were not watching, he frantically tried to clean up the unkempt mess his feathers were. When he realized we were watching him, he raised his head in haughty dignity and gazed out to sea, as though he had not a care in the world, given lie only by the unruly soiled mess of feathers sticking out in all directions. I think he might have heard Ken saying to toss him, as from that day on, he would fly at Ken every time he came close, which left me to tend to him. Cocky, I think, now figured he was the skipper of the upturned dinghy on deck, where he perched, aggressively attacking anyone, other than myself, who approached.

We waited the rest of that day with still no sign of the atoll chief. We had a get-together to discuss the situation. From day one, Antonio the skipper of the factory ship had been trying to dissuade us from continuing on our venture. He kept pointing out that his lifeboats were bigger than our boat (which they were) and saying there was no way we would make it. When Ken hurt his foot on the anchor, Antonio said, almost gleefully, that with such an injury, we could definitely not continue on our journey now. We began to suspect that the skipper of the big ship was colluding with the local chief to stop us from attempting the crossing. Ken and I decided to climb aboard the *Pontevedra*, even though we were barred from doing so, and go on a bit of a fact-finding mission.

While Ken went to talk to Antonio, I went to speak to some of the crew I had become friendly with, especially their engineer, who was also the baker. If they did know something, they weren't giving anything up. I did manage to let them know that no matter what, we were planning to slip away at midnight and that I would be chucking the mooring line then. Ken still wanted to spend time with the skipper, so I told him to give me a shout when he was ready to be picked up and returned to the *Miken*.

As I boarded, Dave pointed out two guys above us, who were astern on the *Pontevedra*. They waved and then frantically beckoned us to bring the *Miken* alongside the factory ship. We could not figure out what they wanted or why, but they were so insistent that we cast off and came alongside the big ship.

The two guys were amidships when they waved at us to stop. We chucked over some fenders to protect us from bumping up against the ship and tied up. Another two guys appeared above, and the four of them surreptitiously passed down something to us over the side.

When it reached us, we saw it was a long hose with the distinct odor of diesel. We wasted little time and filled all our diesel tanks and drums that we had used so far. The guys on deck then pulled up the hose, after which Dave and I climbed up and thanked them profusely, but they pretended to not hear us. They were not to know how much of a lifesaver that was to be. However, we had one more favor to ask as we planned to slip away. Just prior to midnight, the same guys came astern the *Pontevedra*, we cast loose, and we waved them goodbye.

We did not start up the engine immediately but let the current silently carry us away. We had drifted a little more than half a mile away when we heard a shout on the *Pontevedra* - it seemed the skipper had somehow discovered our getaway. We could just make out people running up to the top deck and clearly heard the Captain frantically calling on his radio.

Ken quickly climbed down the *Miken's* engine hatch to fire her up. She kicked over, ran for a while, then died. Ken tried again, then again, but there was no joy. Her engine would not run.

By now, a launch was approaching us at great speed with some somber-looking officials on board. When they came alongside us, Ken wished them a good evening as innocently as he could, while the rest of us pretended to be sleeping. Ken shouted to them that we had just moved away from the factory ship, as we could not sleep because it was too noisy. Then he asked them matter-of-factly what he could do for them. They made some gestures at us, which I thought did not bode well, and then the one who seemed to be in charge waved us off.

"Okay, go, go, you can go!"

It seemed we were free to go!

It was two o'clock in the morning. We had eventually drifted into shallow water, so we dropped the anchor and waited for the morning light so as to check the engine. We discovered one of the tappets was bent, and we worked all morning to repair and reset them.

Dave having a wash on deck.
Note: The plank extending the transom behind him.

.

Next Stop Chagos/
Something Massive in the Way

Extract from journal:

Monday 20th December 1980
Engine repaired. Raised anchor 10.42 hours.
Left Gatdal atoll.
12.45 Two sailfish strikes.
14.10 Outside Wadu island, sea bit rough, next stop
Chagos. Over 1000 sea miles

Days of calm seas followed as our forty-foot boat steadily made its way alone across the ocean. We relaxed, playing board games or cards while listening to music on the radio, the tranquility only interrupted when one of the fishing rods would scream us into action as a big fish took a trailing lure. When the heat got too much for us, we would stop the engine and drift for a while as we dove from the flybridge into the cool sea, after which we would enjoy a hearty lunch in the absolute stillness. Then we would fire up the engine again and head south toward that uninhabited atoll rising out of the Chagos underwater banks in the middle of the Indian Ocean. We would spend our nights on the flybridge with a plate of fresh fish rice, salad, and some fruit along with a mug of coffee complemented with a shot of rationed rum. Then we watched the bow cut through the water that reflected stars so bright they sparkled like diamonds on the calm sea of the Doldrums like a mirror. We would then take our shifts through the night.

The following day, the engine purred as we cut through these flat seas, our reflection distorted in the water by the wake of the bow.

This calm, however, was not to last.

That afternoon, after a morning of blissful cruising, a dark line creeped over the horizon. It slowly became darker and angrier as it rose menacingly into the sky. As we headed closer to the black mass, the seas began to change. The wind picked up, and in the distance, a line of whitecaps came at us with alarming speed. We got ready to face what was obviously a massive storm, though we did not reckon on just how big this storm was to be. This would be a true test for the *Miken*.

The seas were already getting nasty when I went up to the fly bridge for my shift. I had for the most part so far on the trip done both Elisabeth's and my own shifts at the helm, however we would almost always kept each other company while there, in this instance though I said to Elisabeth that I would not only take on her shift through this storm but asked her to baton down with the others in the cabin until the storm abated, this was to be a six-hour roller coaster from hell, both physically and emotionally.

Something massive in the way. A huge storm approaching.
Note: The square jury-rigged sail.

As the night descended, it quickly turned pitch-dark, the black clouds blocking out any starlight. However, I could still make out the first monstrous wave that came at us, along with howling wind and stinging rain. The *Miken* rose up the wave before I could throttle down in time, and we went airborne, hung there for a while, and then plummeted nose-down into the valley behind the wave. My stomach was in my throat as we hit with a sound that suggested the *Miken* had been pounded to pieces. But she amazingly pushed through, coming up while peeling the waves off her bow. This time, I was ready for the next wave. As our boat climbed the crest of the following surge of water I throttled right back and managed to surf the *Miken* down the valley. I had to keep this up, wave after wave. It was impossible to judge each wave, though; every time I heard the screw screaming astern in the air, I knew another free fall was coming. After a few of these poundings, I wondered how much more the *Miken*'s marine plywood could take. My course was generally south, but I mainly just kept the nose to the wind, fearing a wave on the beam would definitely broach us. The screeching wind felt like sandpaper against my face and hands, and the stinging rain and salt water turned my cheeks raw. I had to constantly wipe my eyes to see ahead. After the initial fear subsided and each motion became mechanical, I began to trust in the *Miken* as her 175 horses maternally bob, bob, bobbed ahead, pushing her nose through the sea over and over again.

A couple of hours into the storm, there was a heart-stopping moment when I misjudged a wave badly, and the *Miken* took off this wave sideways. She rocked badly on one side, then bounced to the opposite side. I swung the wheel frantically to straighten her up, praying she would not broach. Just in time, she came around to take the next wave head-on at the bow—*that was close!*

I must admit that this brought the fear back, and for some reason my thoughts went to Elisabeth and her family, our close friends, and of course, my own mother. I had been in many situations where there was an element of danger, always believing a guardian angel watched over us, which Elisabeth had also come to trust in. But were we tempting fate a bit too much here?

I brushed the doubt aside and pumped myself up - I would get through this! But every now and then, the picture in my mind of Elisabeth's family looking at me with stern reproach would creep back. I had to get the emotion in check and believe. Then another emotional bomb hit...

The ladies wanted to heat up a drink for me but trying that in the galley proved impossible in the rough seas. Elisabeth had a small camping Handigas burner, so between her and Nicole, they managed to hold it down in a corner with towels and somehow make a warmish brew of powdered-chocolate drink in a sealed thermos. Dave volunteered to bring the flask up to me...

They say waves come in sets, the last of these being the biggest. I think one of these was on its way as Dave came up the ladder to the flybridge. The screw screamed in the air as I flew off the top of this huge wave. Instead of hitting down in the valley of the wave, we hit this one head-on in the middle of the oncoming mass of water. The bow disappeared into the sea. The wall of water kept coming until it hit as high as the flybridge and rushed over the topside. I spun around in the swivel chair to avoid the force of the water as it came over. Dave was at the top of the ladder with flask in hand, and the wave hit him full-on, knocking him to the lower deck.

Not knowing if he would be swept overboard the *Miken*'s low transom, I screamed over and over, "Man over! Man over!"

I swung back around in the chair to get control of the boat. Unlike a yacht, we had no keel, so I *had* to keep her bow in the wind, and at the same time, reaching for a Dan Buoy on the railing alongside the helm to cast into the sea for Dave without losing control of the wheel. I doubted anyone in the cabin could hear me screaming. I desperately pounded the deck with my feet. This became one of the worst moments in the entire venture, if indeed in my entire lifetime.

What do I do? If Dave went overboard, do I turn around and look for him in the dark water? And in the process, risk all our lives in possibly broaching in the high seas? And in doing so, possibly turning the boat beam on the waves, in which case we would more than likely go over. It even crossed my mind how I would explain this to his family.

I was sitting with one of the worst decisions in my life, and I had to make it soon. I have been known to take some chances at times throughout my life, but was this a chance too far? Sophie's choice was staring me in the face, and Dave could be drifting in the sea, farther away each second. Do I get through the storm, then turn back doing the standard figure-eight search pattern - or do I turn now?

I found myself screaming into the wind at the storm, at God, or nothing in particular, just screaming. Then I heard a voice scream back at me. Was that Dave in the water, screaming back?

I yelled his name, and with enormous relief, heard him say, "I'm okay! I'm okay!" He was on the lower deck!

Dave told me later (with another warm cup of much-welcomed hot chocolate) that the plank we used to extend the transom stopped him from going over. I was spared from having to make that terrible choice, but it haunted me throughout the rest of the storm, and days after. Later on, when the seas were calm and I was alone on deck, I thought maybe that guardian angel was not so fanciful after all, and I let it go.

The wind subsided toward the last hour of my shift, and the Indian Ocean quietened down to choppy seas. I retired from my shift, stunned and amazed that we had survived those hours of constant, pounding punishment.

However, I was exhausted. Ken's bunk was still pretty dry, so he offered it to me. I gratefully accepted and escaped into a deep sleep.

Some hours later, I awoke to a tranquil sea. The sky was clear, and the sun shone with the promise of a wonderful day. But we had a lot of mess to sort out. Everybody was busy on deck. Worryingly, even though we had hung the bags in plastic, much of our supplies still got soaked. We laid our wet provisions out on the deck to dry it off and see how much of the rice, flour, oats, and sugar we could save. The cabin and galley were in shambles.

Paradise, our mongoose companion, had hunkered down in a cupboard during the storm, so it was decided to leave him where he was. Sadly, he must have landed hard during the pounding of the storm, as he did not survive. I was going to miss our friendly, mischievous bundle of energy and his company with us at the helm.

The chickens, however, survived, and Cocky was soon back on his perch, proud as ever on the upturned dinghy.

Later, Nicole tried her hand at fishing and proudly caught her first fish, a fat bonito. So, she tried to make us meals with the wet supplies of rice and flour the best she could to accompany her fish. This would last for a while, but we had to dump most of these supplies later. The day after the storm, we arrived in the Doldrums, which yachtsmen generally hate, as they come completely becalmed here, and their boats just sit under a scorching sun, going nowhere, sometimes for weeks. I have heard stories of sailors losing their minds in the Doldrums and actually walking off their boats. However, for us in a motorboat, the Doldrums couldn't be better for a couple of reasons: we had an engine and not sails to move, we saved on fuel in these calm seas, and we were navigating on a sextant.

The islands we were looking for were small and flat, the highest point being a palm tree. If there was any swell, it would be easy to miss them. However, the Doldrums gave us sight to the horizon and a much better chance of finding them. We stopped the *Miken* and turned off her engine for a while to enjoy our lunch as we drifted peacefully on the quiet sea. However, without even the slightest breeze, the sun beat down on us from both above and the reflected rays off the sea below. So, after the meal, we dove overboard to cool off in the deep, blue ocean.

Later as we restarted the engine to continue on our way, there was a noticeable shudder coming up from the shaft of the boat. Had the pounding of the storm bent it? Ken was a bit anxious about it but decided it was not too serious. That night, the steering failed.

We checked the cable, expecting it to be the same problem we had when motoring past the Great Basque ridge off Sri Lanka, but the cable appeared to be in working order. Ken swore, for if the fault was what he suspected, then we were in bad trouble. We rushed to the stern to check the rudder itself, where Ken's worst fear was confirmed: it had snapped clean off. So, the storm had left its mark after all.

Amazingly, the rudder had not fallen away, and Ken wanted to salvage it. I dove under to see that it was being held by a single pin in a ring. I figured Dave and I could lift it out if Ken and the ladies could take the strain on a rope. We could then climb back on board and help them lift it up. We knew the rudder was heavy, so with Ken's assurance that he would take the weight topside, Dave and I took to the water.

We dove below to the base of the rudder, tied the rope around it, then surfaced to tell Ken we were going to dive down and lift it out. He gave us the thumbs-up.

At first, we struggled because it was so heavy, and we had to make a few attempts. Finally, with great effort, we lifted the rudder out, but as it came clear, the weight of it caused Dave and me to plummet with it into the depth. As it turned out, Ken had been so busy talking to the ladies that he let the rope go. Fortunately, the rope was anchored, and we finally came to a halt pretty deep underwater. Kicking hard, Dave and I thrashed for the surface to find Ken looking down at us sheepishly making profuse apologies. Dave told him what he thought in emphatic terms!

I climbed on board first, then turned to give Dave a hand when something behind him caught my eye. It was the unmistakable fin of a huge shark coming at speed.

"Get out! Shark!" I shouted.

Dave grabbed my hand and nearly yanked me in as well, but I held him as he scrambled on board.

A massive great white shark came alongside and cruised around, its big black eye staring at us. The shark hung around for quite a while. I was not sure if it was curious or hungry, but both Dave and I were more than relieved it had not shown up a few moments earlier.

Between us all, we managed to haul the rudder aboard, though it was, in fact, useless to us. We had no underwater welding equipment to repair a stainless-steel rudder. It was here that Ken's prophecy about blessing the plank again came true. We used it to try to construct a jury-rigged rudder.

We drilled some holes in the plank above and below, and then pushed rope through the holes to balance it between the stern railings. The shark was no longer in sight, but we had to get into the sea at times to set the plank "rudder." Knowing a great white could come unseen from deep below, we had some anxious moments.

Well, the new rudder pushed us along. There was only one snag, though. We tended to go around and around in circles. No matter which way we moved the plank, we would either go around to port, or around to starboard. We just could not get it to push us forward for any length of time. I was up at the helm when, for the umpteenth time, Ken and Dave tried another adjustment. I then opened the throttle, and this time we did move forward for a while, but eventually, we slowly came to port again. In exasperation, I throttled down immediately, and the *Miken* swung to starboard on the deceleration.

"Whoa!" I called to the guys. "Check this out."

So, we left the plank as is and started to play with the throttle, accelerating and decelerating. Doing this, we found we could actually steer in a desired direction, kind of zigzagging our way along, across the vast Indian Ocean!

Our jury-rigged plank rudder.

Here was another reason why we were lucky to be in the calm seas of the Doldrums. As we all were aware, this probably would not have worked in rough seas.

I think it is pertinent to mention at this stage how things were going between all of us on the *Miken*. Other than the usual good-humored banter and Ken's maniacal excitement when we were fishing, the mood between us was positive, and we got on well together. The ladies were still very upbeat, trusting we would get them through. Ken was the type of man who pretty much thrived on this sort of thing.

I must admit, ventures like this made me feel alive. However, after the storm and the loss of our rudder, Dave did come to me on the fly bridge and voice his concerns. He figured that we were now in big trouble, and what did I think our chances were of finding the islands?

It was the first time I had heard genuine worry in his voice. I said as long as we had calm seas and fuel in the tank, we still had a chance. I went on to say there was also a chance we might see a ship and fire a flare for help, as I reckoned most of these big ships would have the means and equipment to repair our rudder. We did have a line-of-sight radio as well. However, I knew we were not in the main shipping lanes, and since leaving the Maldives, we had been alone with no other ship in sight.

The words were hardly out my mouth when Dave and I simultaneously spotted a dot on the horizon. It was a ship. We got on the radio and called ship-to-ship on the usual channel 16. There was no response, so we tried other channels. Still no response. We kept trying, but no matter how much we called, if they could hear us, they did not reply. Ken wanted to save as many flares as he could, but he reckoned if we shot a flare and still had no response, then we could figure the ship was not responding because they thought we were pirates. We did see three other ships far in the distance that day, and the response - or, should I say, lack thereof - was the same from all of them. We were on our own. We did know this could well be the case before we left on this adventure. Dave came from a place where, if one was in trouble at sea, everybody would come to your assistance if they were able to. So, this did not go down well with him, and his mood worsened.

This did not improve when we took our midday sun-shot with the sextant the following day; it appeared that we were quite a bit off course.

We were undecided if this was due to our new steering mechanism or if our compass was faulty again—or both. Perhaps our sun-shot reading had been incorrect. Ken said it couldn't be the compass again, though we all knew it had to be. Dave pointed out that the compass was mounted next to the wheel, which was made of iron and could affect the readings. He had a point. So, we brought this to Ken's attention, who dismissed it and said it had never been a problem in the past. Whatever it was, we decided to go easy on our water supply. There was no sign of the Chagos Bank or the Peros Banhos Atoll, and now we were getting low on fuel.

Late that afternoon, we had an exciting distraction. The reel screamed in protest as yards and yards of line dragged away. I grabbed the rod and hit the fish. He was on!

Dave was at the wheel, so Ken and Nicole rushed down to reel in the lines of the other two rods as I fought the fish. Ken asked if the fish felt like a big one. The line was coming in fairly easily, so I replied, "Not so big."

The words were hardly out of my mouth when, as if to prove me wrong, the rod jerked down. I leaned with all my weight against it as, once again, yards and yards of line was dragged from the reel. This was a *very* big fish.

An hour later, my aching arms felt as if they had been nearly wrenched from their sockets, but at last the fish was close enough for us to get eyes on it.

Ken cried out in excitement, "Yellowfin tuna! Look at the size of it! It has to be a world record!"

I was really feeling the strain on my burning muscles, but this news gave me an extra surge of energy. For the next ten minutes, I fought hard to bring the tuna within lassoing distance. The big fish was almost "home" when it suddenly dashed across the boat, wrapping the line around our jury rudder. Ken tried to get the line free, but the rod bounced up in my hands, as the line snapped against the rough edge of the plank.

Ken patted me on the shoulder. "Tough luck, Gordon. That was by far the biggest yellowfin I've ever seen!"

We watched the fish going up and down on the surface. It, too, was exhausted. I grabbed my spear gun, and for one insane moment, I considered going in after it. Elisabeth looked at me with a "really?" look on her face, and the moment passed. We watched the massive tuna recover and swim away.

And that's my story of the big one that got away.

Late that afternoon, I had an amusing and, later to be proven, profound experience. While I was taking my shift, a gannet-like seabird - I believe it was a booby - appeared out of nowhere, circled the *Miken*, and then hitched a ride on the sunshade canvas. It had webbed feet, so it struggled to land, but after making a few undignified attempts, it finally landed with a thump and waddled to the corner, where it made itself at home. I wondered what he was doing way out here alone, but I was glad for the company. I relaxed in the helm chair, listening to some pleasant music over a set of earphones as the sun disappeared over the ocean.

I found a bright star in the sky and placed it beside the jury mast for an easy navigation point. On one occasion, a combination of the music, the moonlit night, and the beauty of the surrounding sea caused my mind to wander, and the star slightly with it. As this happened and the compass needle moved off course, the head of the booby appeared upside down over the edge of the canvas, looked me up and down, and squawked angrily. This impressed me so much that I called Elisabeth to join me at the helm to witness this. Then I purposely went off our course. The bird reacted in the same way every time.

The following day, the sun rose on a flat sea with not a breath of wind. Our wayward hitchhiker had gone on his way. I walked onto the deck with a mug of tea in my hand to see an amazing sight unfold in the daylight: hundreds of spinner dolphins were jumping and spinning in the air around us. They appeared to be frolicking just for the sheer joy of it, which was kind of infectious and put us all in a good mood. I liked to think they were putting on a show just for us, and for some inexplicable reason, this made me feel we would all make it to the islands okay.

In the near-midday heat of that morning, Cocky must have decided he wanted to cool off, and without a word to anybody, jumped overboard. We had no way of steering directly to him, and our jury rudder disallowed reverse. We had seen several sharks around earlier, so we were not overenthusiastic about swimming for him. So, for a while, we all stood and watched the ridiculous sight of a cockerel paddling madly for his life after a boat in the middle of the Indian Ocean.

Ken said, "He's your bird, Gordon. I'm not going after him."

"That makes two of us," said Dave.

I had become quite fond of Cocky, so I attempted to break the two-hundred-yard freestyle record. I dove overboard and went after him. Then, using him like a water polo ball, albeit a flapping and squawking one, I swam back to the boat with the cockerel between my arms and threw him on board. Here, on behalf of Cocky the cockerel, we would like to claim another first, for I doubt any other chicken has gone for a swim in the middle of the Indian Ocean.

When Cocky had settled down, I relieved Ken at the wheel while Dave kept me company.

We were now five days out from the Maldives. Ken had us change course several times with still no sign of the islands or the Chagos Bank. Dave turned to me. He was angry now.

"That's eight times we've changed course the last two days," he said, "I'm not sure Ken's navigation skills are that good, because I reckon we're lost!"

He went on to point out that the jury rig rudder was making us zigzag, and so the fuel was running out. He also pointed out the water would not last forever. We had chased a couple of squalls and, using the canvas, made a catchment to fill our water containers. But if we ran out of fuel and had no power, we would have to rely on rain squalls coming to us and be at the complete mercy of the sea. We had seen no other vessel for the past two days, and if there were ships in the area, they most likely would not come to our aid. Dave knew this situation was dire. Ken was below at the navigation table when he called to Dave. A little while later, Dave returned and said with frustration, "Ken wants to try another course!"

I said, "No, tell Ken I'm staying on this heading." I understand there is only one skipper on a boat, but I had my reasons. Dave went down to let him know.

Ken bounded up the ladder to the fly bridge. "What do you mean you won't change course!"

"Ken," I responded quietly. "You have changed course several times now. We need to stay in one direction for a while so we can hopefully hit the banks, and we'll get our bearings there. I have a three-hour shift. I want to stay on this course until my shift is over."

Ken considered this. "You know our fuel is running out. Are you prepared to live with that decision?"

"I am," I said simply. Elisabeth was the only one who knew why I wanted to stay on that particular heading. It was on this exact heading where the seabird hitchhiker was happy.

A navigator has to take into account the lee and drift, as currents and wind can move you off course. I was aware of this, but still stayed on the exact course the bird was happy with.

Dave stayed to give me some company at the helm. The sea was so flat and calm we could scan all the way to the horizon.

Instantaneously, we both spotted a tiny dot appear where the sea joined the sky.

"Looks like a ship," I said.

Dave looked at it for a while. "Gordon, you know, I think that's a f—ing island!"

Wishful thinking, I thought. "Nah, it's a ship," I said cautiously. "Watch, it'll sail away."

Dave rushed below decks to find the binoculars and was back in flash, focusing them on the spot in the distance. "There is a palm tree! I can see a f—ing palm tree!" he cried out jubilantly.

Indeed, far off to our starboard was a small, lonely island—a needle in a vast, watery haystack. The day was the twenty-fifth, the month was December, and before us lay one of the best Christmas gifts I have ever received. One could accuse Elisabeth and myself of being fanciful here, but both of us do believe our feathered hitchhiker that came out of nowhere was more than just circumstance.

Dave grabbed some mugs, poured some leftover rum, and we celebrated this tiny little island in the middle of the ocean, two thousand miles from Sri Lanka and two thousand still from Kenya, just about as far from civilization as one could possibly get. I secretly toasted a wayward seabird and any guardian angel that may have sent him.

Dave was beaming. It was good to see his positive attitude back again. The ladies were kind of philosophical about it all. "Oh, we knew. We never doubted you guys," said Nicole, in a matter-of-fact manner. Ken was also in good spirits, as he joined us to celebrate with the last of the rum.

Just before sunset, we left the deep, blue water; entered into the shallow, green waters of the banks; and anchored off the island.

Needle in a watery haystack. Tiny island spotted on Christmas Day.
Celebrating with a mug of rum.

The following morning, the euphoria of the previous day was now tempered with reality.

We identified the half-mile-long island from the charts as being one of three called the "Brothers." So, at least now we knew where we were. However, I reckoned this island was too small for us to survive on. Even the coconut palm trees were few, and obviously the island had no water. I voiced my opinion in this regard.

Dave became quite agitated. He wanted to get off! We had been onboard the *Miken* for twenty-one days straight now, and I think he just wanted terra firma.

Ken turned to me. "Gordon, you're the survivalist. Do you think we have any chance of surviving on that island?"

"No way," I replied. "We have to see if we can reach the Peros Banhos Atoll. We know people have tried to live there in the distant past. It's also where the pile of diesel fuel had been discovered, according to your yachtie friends."

"Okay," said Ken. "Let's see how far it is and work out if we have enough fuel to get there."

Ken checked the charts.

The Great Chagos Bank is considered one of the largest archipelagos in the world, and perhaps the most pristine. However, most of it is submerged with very few islands rising above it. This one was one of them. There are seven atolls surrounding Chagos that have islands above the watermark. The area is huge (approximately a thousand square miles), so these atolls are quite far from each other.

While anchored in the transparent, shallow green water over the coral, one has the illusion of being safe rather than out in the deep blue. Perhaps because it is possible to see the bottom below. But that's just, of course, an illusion.

Peros Banhos Atoll consists of twenty-nine islands. It has been described as one of the most remarkable in the world and likened to an emerald necklace misplaced by the gods. Ken figured the atoll was ninety miles northeast of our position. To reach it, we would have to leave our little island and head back into the deep.

After Ken had measured our fuel, he calculated that, if the sea remained calm, we had just enough left to get there.

However, Ken figured it was a gamble with fuel that low, so even he, as the skipper, decided not to make the decision but to put it to a vote. One could see Dave was loath to leave the land, even if it was just this small island.

I pointed out that the island would just be a prison and eventually a death trap. It was worth the risk to get to the Peros Banhos Atoll, as it was our best hope of surviving.

Dave reminded us that no modern-day ship plied these waters, and even the few yachts that sailed through here went further east. So, should we not make it, we could not expect any rescue or help at all. We would be out here alone.

Dave was, of course, correct in that regard. There was a real danger that our reliable *Miken* could become our prison and demise instead. Dave looked over at the lonely, picturesque island we had been so elated to find—now just to leave it? Elisabeth and Nicole voted to go. Dave looked at us, and then reluctantly agreed. "Guess we don't have a choice," he conceded.

"Okay," said Ken. "Let's up anchor and go for it!"

I must admit, as we left the green water and headed out into the deep blue again, it was somewhat scary. For a moment, I empathized with Dave, and wondered if it would be better to take our chances on the island instead of being adrift on this boat in this vast, empty ocean. The hours passed slowly as the last of our diesel got lower and lower. We dreaded to hear the engine cough as it starved for fuel.

In the late afternoon, I was on the lower deck with Ken as he checked the fuel level. He estimated we had only four hours' steaming left. For the first time, I could see despair and real worry in his eyes. I looked past him over the bow and tried to contain my excitement. "Ken, look!"

Ken turned to see a string of islands appear on the horizon. And there was Peros Banhos Atoll, rising out of the sea before us. He punched his fist into the air. "Yes! Yes! Yes!" he yelled with relief in his voice, and I am certain I saw a tear or two in his eyes. We heard a lot of stomping, whooping, and shouting above deck as Elisabeth, Nicole, and Dave had obviously spotted the islands as well. We had made it!

Made it! Entering Paros Banhos Atoll

Ken took the helm and told Dave and I to put out all five fishing rods. His plan was to head straight for the atoll, then run parallel with the islands and see how the fishing was along the reefs. I doubt if the fish here had ever seen a net, let alone a lure.

As we came alongside the reef, there was a sudden cacophony of noise, as all five reels screamed in unison. It was pandemonium! Initially, we thought we had hit a shoal of tuna, but we were hauling in many different species of fish. It became so hectic we had to remove rods and concentrate only on two. Even then, we still had our hands full.

Sixty Pound Wahoo landed by Gordon.

The lures were not even reaching beyond the propeller's white water. One fish, a large sixty-pound wahoo, came clear of the water using its superior speed, and hit a lure from above to get at it first. Ken, who had fished professionally for twenty-five years, declared he had never seen anything like this. Not even close. After an amazing stint of fishing, we checked the charts for a passage into the lagoon of the atoll. We continued along the reef until we eventually found it. We entered into the lagoon waters, looking for a particular island, Île du Coin (or Corner Island). According to our research, this was the island that had been deserted and, most importantly, where the supposed pile of diesel drums was hidden in the jungle.

Fifteen minutes from the gap, we spotted an island up ahead that looked three miles long and a mile wide. A while later, we spotted the top of a rusty old roof just showing above the jungle growth, indicating this must be Île du Coin.

Being the largest of all the twenty-nine islands in the atoll, Île du Coin was the only island that had inhabitants at some point. A couple of ships had run aground on this archipelago in the early 1500s, but those castaways all perished. The first people ever to inhabit the island was in 1556, when a ship wrecked on the outer reef. Over a hundred survivors made it to this island. There were very few coconut palms then, which could have provided water and food. However, they did find water by digging shallow wells. There had been thousands of birds on the island, and many turtles came to the beaches to lay their eggs. Unfortunately, the birds and turtles were nearly all killed for food, resulting in most of these survivors eventually dying from hunger as well.

The islands became part of the British territory in 1814. Prior to that, around 1793, the islands had belonged to the French, who brought slaves to the Chagos Islands to plant coconut palms for the copra it produces. The main settlement was at Diego Garcia's largest island on the other side of the Chagos Bank, about two hundred nautical miles away from this atoll. There, a relatively larger population was established, and this island is now an important US military base. Peros Banhos was more of a plantation outpost with very few people. Later, when synthetic fibers were invented, the copra market collapsed, and with the nearest mainland being two thousand miles away, it was no longer viable to continue. So, the few inhabitants working here were translocated, either to Mauritius or the Seychelles.

We hoped to find things those people had left behind so as to help us survive here. Although none of us mentioned it, we all knew that if there were no full diesel drums hidden in the jungle, we would all now be stranded on this uninhabited, deserted island in the middle of the Indian Ocean.

But first, we all stood on deck to admire the beauty of the islands surrounding the lagoon, the blue water changing to turquoise and eventually emerald green as it rested on snow-white beaches fringed by coconut palms.

We did not know it then, but this lonely island was to become our home for quite some time.

As we motored closer, we noticed a broken-down old jetty leading from the beach about a third of the way to the northern side of the island. We wondered if we could reach it by boat to use as a mooring.

We knew that the few yachtsmen who sailed way out here would never come to this atoll. The charts discouraged it, saying the large twelve-mile lagoon did not offer safe anchorage, whereas another smaller atoll two hundred miles further east, the Salomon, offered good anchorage. So, if they came this way at all, they would head for that atoll instead. Finding safe anchorage, of course, was of great concern to Ken as well, as the *Miken* was practically all he had to his name.

Unfortunately, with the passing of the years, coral and sand had completely reclaimed the area about the old jetty. There was no way any boat could get even close to it now. So, no chance of mooring there.

In fact, it became evident that we would have to drop anchor over a mile from the beach, where there was water shallow enough for our anchor ropes to reach. A twelve-mile lagoon can still build up a big sea, and if the *Miken* swung on the ropes, the coral reef would chew her to pieces. This did not sit well with Ken, and we now understood the charts warning of bad anchorage in this atoll.

Our Island Home

Elisabeth entered in the log:

26th December 1980 arrived safely at Peros Banhos
Less than 4 hours fuel left in the tanks
Zig sagging used more than expected
Thankful to the crew of Pontevedra
The islands are beautiful, looking forward to getting off
the boat and feel some ground under my feet
> *We have enough daylight left to go exploring*
> *Can't wait*

With the *Miken* anchored, we all launched the dinghy, climbed aboard, and rowed toward the beach. Below us, in crystal-clear water, lay solid coral reef. A kaleidoscope of color and marine life passed below us. I could barely contain the urge to take a deep breath and dive overboard. However, the island needed exploring first.

Beyond the main reef was a stretch of isolated patches of coral and sand, which eventually gave way to about a hundred yards of white, sandy bottom all the way up to the beach.

We stepped ashore onto the soft, sandy beach partially shaded by coconut palms, some of which stood a good seventy feet tall. I was glad to see these were king coconut, which I had discovered in Sri Lanka were considered the best of all coconuts. Behind the palms, a jungle of vines awaited us. We battled our way through the foliage to where we had seen the rusty roof and soon came upon the first structure on the island.

In essence, it was just a corrugated iron roof about thirty yards long and ten yards wide. It was propped up to a height of about twelve feet by fourteen stout concrete pillars. Other than the roof, it was completely overgrown.

Not far from this building, we uncovered another large-walled shed, which may have been used for stores. Beside it, was what looked like a workshop. Inside this building, we found materials that in any civilized place would be considered junk, but to us was quite a find. We found a few old tools, rolls of wire, and various other useful-looking items.

We decided to make a clearing before the sun set and build a fire. Exploring the rest of the island could wait until morning.

After collecting what we needed from the boat for the night, we made a simple meal of fish and rice over the fire and canned peaches as a well-earned treat, followed by a small tot of arrack to celebrate. As we sat around the fire, there was a good deal of laughing, joking, and good humor, as the tense load of the past few days dissipated. A couple of hours later, this was replaced with a feeling of absolute exhaustion. While Ken, Nichole, and Dave found places to bed down, Elisabeth and I found a spot on the beach beside the lagoon, lay under the starlight in each other's arms, and drifted off to sleep.

Early the next morning, we all gathered under the large roof of the shed to enjoy a breakfast of oats and coconut. Afterward, we made a rationed cup of coffee and sat together to discuss our situation.

We agreed that we couldn't make a decision until we knew if there really was diesel on the island. Ken reckoned he could build a wooden tiller rudder, which could be controlled from the stern. However, if there was no diesel, we were going nowhere, and the chances of us being found here anytime soon were remote. Ken said that no modern-day ship had been in these immediate waters for decades, and it was highly unlikely any yacht that might come this way would arrive at this atoll. We would then, at least for the time being, have to assume that was the case, and that we could be here for some time to come. We would have to ration the supplies we had left, much of which the big storm had already ruined.

Ken was unquestionably the skipper aboard the *Miken*, but not here on the island. There was no disrespect intended. Although we still needed to make a communal decision, I was glad to get some of my independence back. So, I suggested that I explore the island to see if I could discover the said pile of diesel drums, then we could make a more informed decision on what we should do.

Ken agreed that was a good idea, and Dave said he would join me. So, Ken decided that the ladies would help him clear the undergrowth under this open shed and clear a path to the water's edge. This would allow us to have a place to bring and store our remaining provisions. Dave and I set off into the small jungle. Cutting our way through the vines, we came to a clearing, where there lay the remains of what must have been small huts. It did not take much imagination to figure this must have been the slave quarters. We continued on. After a while as we approached the middle of the island, we spotted another red corrugated roof quite high above the undergrowth. We worked our way toward it and came on a large, partly hidden, double-story wooden house, complete with top-story balconies. This must have been the overseer's house.

The spooky wooden mansion in the jungle.

Note: Daves' maize crop growing in the foreground.

In its day, this mini mansion must have been a grand place for a small island like this. Whomever had lived there must have lived like a king, albeit of a tiny kingdom. Dave and I found a way into the house, but it immediately became evident that the house was rotted through, which made it a potential death trap. Any thoughts of living in this house were quickly dispelled when I attempted to climb the inside stairway and the whole structure nearly came down on top of me. After that, we treaded carefully.

In the house, we found some old cupboards, a table, and the base of a double bed, which I claimed for Elisabeth and myself.

Dave and I left the old house to later return for the furniture, and we continued to explore the island.

Not long afterward, another opening revealed a simple graveyard with a handful of graves. Just beyond this was a single-cell jailhouse. I am not sure what crimes would have been committed back then, but with just a single jail cell, it could not have been much. Although, it did make me wonder, and it was sobering to think, that even a beautiful place like this a prison was needed. The contradiction of a jailhouse in paradise was not lost on us.

After some hours with no sign of any diesel drums, we decided to head back to the others for lunch.

On our return, Ken and the ladies were hard at work and had cleared a fair amount of the vines and growth from under the shed. Ken looked at us inquiringly as we approached. We shook our heads and shrugged before he could ask if we had found the diesel, but we still had a lot of the island to cover.

After a lunch break, Dave and I joined in to clean up what we now called our "Clubhouse." We divided the shed into a kitchen area (where Ken dug a fire pit), as well as a dining and lounging area. Dave then went to the boat to collect the cane chairs. Elisabeth, Nicole, and I returned to the old wooden house to get the table and cupboards there. It was worth the struggle to get them back to the shed. Dave had left the cane chairs on the beach to go back to the boat for other supplies, so Elisabeth and I slashed open the pathway leading from the shed to the beach and brought up the chairs to our new "Clubhouse."

The 'Clubhouse' after it had been cleared of jungle growth.

Ken knew I had brought my diving gear and spear gun with me, and as we had flayed and salted the fish, we had caught he asked if I would get us a fresh fish for supper. So, while the others off-loaded more of the supplies, I headed for the lagoon with my spear gun. This was to become the most reliable way of getting food in the days to come.

Dave offloading our cane chairs onto the island.

I swam out to the sandy area, where I saw several stingrays. Although I knew from when I had lived in the Caribbean that they are good eating, I decided to leave them for now. Past the sandy area, I reached the corals.

The ocean was clear to the bottom, and before me appeared so much marine life of every conceivable color in intricate patterns and contrasts that I did not know where to look. There were bright orange, red, and yellow butterfly or tangfish, the navy blue of the blue king angelfish with its black facemask, bright-yellow dorsal fin, and cream-white tail and pectoral fins. Different-colored parrot fish, some with light or dark-blue and green colors molding into each other; others a dark green and crimson or orange. Various angelfish striped with pink, red, violet, orange, blue, green, white, or black; the soft yellow of the damselfish with their black sergeant-major stripes; wrasse and surgeonfish spotted or striped in a medley of colors. Triggerfish waved about like foreign flags and purple-spotted groupers and bass in different shades. Amongst this colorful marine life, the coral gardens Mother Nature had taken centuries to build resulted in a brilliant wonder world that only she and time could achieve. This was a diver's paradise. These were virgin, untouched coral reefs that I doubt had seen a diver in decades, and I had it all to myself.

I had lost track of time when I saw a blacktip shark come out of the blue water and chase a shoal of mullet to catch his supper, which reminded me why I was here. I remembered that I had my underwater camera back at camp, so I was looking forward to see if I could capture a glimpse of this beautiful underwater garden and its teeming life, but that would have to wait. There would be plenty of time later to come recreational diving. Right now, I needed food for the camp.

It wasn't long before a fair-sized grouper emerged from his underwater cave, about forty feet below. I dove down and got a good shot on him, then immediately looked around for the shark. Sure enough, he was bearing down on me with a white tip shark not far behind him. I was not going to let them have my fish, so I chased the sharks off and headed back to the beach.

When I came out of the water with the decent-sized fish, Ken was waiting for me with a big smile on his face. (Ken really liked his food!) "Nice one, Gordon! I will clean that for you," he said.

Ken cleaning Gordons speared grouper for supper.
Note: Plastic bag on Ken's injured foot.

Ken had put a new plastic bag over his injured foot, which still had not healed properly, and I mentioned it. He said the bandages were all used up. We still had some topical antibiotics and hydrogen peroxide, but this was somewhat of a concern, as in the tropics, even a small wound can get badly infected with serious consequences.

We spent the next morning off-loading our remaining provisions. We decided that, because we would all be meeting, cooking, eating and spending time at the Clubhouse, we should make it as clean as possible. Once that was done, we hauled up beach sand and placed it over the brown ground of the Clubhouse until we had a carpet of clean, white sand. We fashioned brooms and brushes from old palms and smoothed it out. It took up the best part of the day, but when we were done, it made quite a difference. We used wooden boxes to keep our food provisions safe from rats.

Nicole asked us to bring any books we had, and she made a "library" using one of the cupboards we had found. She also placed our board games and playing cards there. The cane chairs were placed round the table we had rescued from the old mansion in the "living room." Utensils, crockery, mugs, pots, and pans were all placed neatly in their own particular place. The kitchen area was also covered with clean, white sand. Here, Ken made a neat fire pit and fashioned a hot-plate surface over it so we could utilize the small, portable wood stove, Chinese wok, and cast-iron pot we had brought with us. When done, the Clubhouse really did look quite comely and comfortable.

Elisabeth had cleared the foliage facing the lagoon, so we had a clear and wonderful view of the beach. She had also noticed some wildflowers around, so she set about to make a small flower bed in front of the Clubhouse just to add to the effect.

Before: Ken building our spot for the kitchen at the Clubhouse.

After: The kitchen Ken built. Note the carpet of clean beach sand.

With Dave's help, I brought the bed base from the old house to the Clubhouse. As luck would have it, our mattress from the boat was a perfect fit, so for the first few days, Elisabeth and I slept there. Ken and Nicole decided to make the "workshop" hut their place to sleep. This suited Ken, as he was really concerned about his boat, and the hut gave him an uninterrupted view of the *Miken* sitting on her anchorage.

Dave still slept onboard, saying he would look for a place for himself later.

Shelter finished; our next concern was water. There are few trees in the world as useful as a coconut - both for food, water, and building material. Any green coconut contains a full mug of water, and the king coconut contains even more. However, most of the palms on this island were between fifty and seventy feet tall, and it takes a certain skill to be able to climb them (I have succeeded only once on a much lower palm that still took the skin off my chest). Belt climbing is an option if we got desperate, but it is dangerous if you slip, which could result in serious injury or death, and there was no ambulance to call out on a deserted island in the middle of the Indian Ocean. There were plenty of dropped coconuts, though most were dried up. Of course, the best chance for water would be rain, especially as we could use the roofs as water catchments. However, we had not seen any squalls for some days now. I knew how to make an evaporation sheet with seawater, but it is slow and tedious, (though this would also double up to make us some sea salt). We could make a similar setup to catch early-morning dew with the classic water-pit funnel design. There were reportedly a few wells on the island, though we had not come across any yet.

Elisabeth wanted to go exploring to see what the island had to offer in the way of food. So, I joined her to go foraging.

We found a few guava trees partially suffocated by vines of wild beans. Each tree had a few miserable-looking green guavas. Farther down the island was a clump of banana trees, but unfortunately, there was only one bunch of small, green bananas between them. We did find, however, some very large breadfruit trees, and each bore the promise of a good crop of fruit, with some ready to pick.

On our way back to the camp, we chanced upon a solitary rosebush with one delightful pink rose in full bloom. There were other flowers as well, the most common being hibiscus. Elisabeth picked some of these to brighten up the Clubhouse.

The following week were days of discovery. On my part, exploring the corals for the best spots to spearfish was my first priority, as it was my task to supply the camp with food from the sea.

I have found when spearfishing at different reefs that the reef seems to "know" if you are too active in one area and the marine life reacts there accordingly, becoming skittish and even vacant to a degree. In the Caribbean, while diving with the locals, I had encouraged the divers to avoid this by quartering the reefs into just one-week dives in one area, then move to another area the next week, and so on, then returning to the first area four weeks later. By that time, I found that part of the reef had recovered and "relaxed again." (When I returned to the Caribbean years later, they were still practicing that quartering system there). I decided to do the same here.

As it was, no two dives were ever the same.

On my next dive, I caught a small hawksbill turtle. This was food like anything else, but it was a turtle, so I took it back to camp and said that if I kill it, all must agree. At that stage, we were not that desperate for a change of diet, and none of us had the heart to kill it, so I set him free. Almost every day from then on, I saw that turtle on my dives. I busted some clams for him, and he soon came to follow me around, even diving down with me on occasion. Because of his wrinkled appearance, we called him "Granddad."

I still needed a fish for supper, so I went out to the blue water and speared a big snapper down deep. He was a powerful fish, and I nearly lost the tug-of-war against him, but with my lungs about to burst, I brought him to the surface, where already an audience of sharks were coming to investigate. They kept their distance, however, so I made my way back to the beach. Coming in, I noticed below me the telltale feelers of a lobster protruding from under a coral head, so I secured the snapper and dove after it.

With my second prize in my hand, I turned to kick to the surface when my heart skipped a beat as I stared into the beady eyes of a gray reef shark. I quickly searched the surrounding water to find two other sharks circling around me. They had followed me in and were now certainly not keeping their distance. One was a four-foot blacktip, the other a six-foot lemon shark. The snapper I killed had obviously attracted them. Well, I was not about to hand over our supper - they could catch their own - so, keeping an eye on them, I flipped slowly back to shore. They watched me go, and on that occasion, never bothered me further.

Sharks were to harass me on every single spearfishing dive. It is well known that sharks can detect minute traces of blood in the water, but the blood has to get to them first. These sharks were undoubtedly being attracted by the thrashing vibrations of the fish I speared, and this being an atoll, it was attracting both the reef and the deep-water oceanic sharks. I had to come up with a plan.

I tied my fish to a polystyrene float I found on the beach and dragged it behind me. This helped from a safety aspect but would cost me fish at times, as my fish became shark food. Every so often, Elisabeth would row out with me on the dinghy, and I would hand her any fish I speared, getting it out of the water as quickly as possible. This worked quite well while we had the dinghy.

It is worth noting that when any of us just went swimming or shelling on the lagoon side of the island, we would often see sharks in the distance, but they would never bother us. However, this was not the case on the open seaside. Here, there was an abundance of oceanic white (silver) tip sharks that would appear quite quickly even if I did not have a fish and hung around as if waiting for me to spear a fish. Some were quite cheeky. So, even though the ocean side was by far the best for spearfishing, I had to limit my dives there, as it became pointless. I would just lose my fish to the sharks. And due to the waves and currents, we could not risk taking the dinghy out there, as there was a real danger of losing it to the currents in the open ocean.

That night, we enjoyed fresh lobster with a special sauce that Nicole prepared, followed up by snapper grilled with garlic. Ken admitted he was not a great fan of diving or spearfishing, so would leave that to me. Dave, though, said he was very keen to give it a try. Also, Ken's foot had not healed, which would not allow him into the sea for a while. So, Ken suggested that he and Dave explore the island further and hopefully find the diesel.

Ken and Dave set out the next day to see what they could discover. They did not find the diesel, but they did discover some lime, orange, more breadfruit trees and some trees with cucumber fruit.

Cucumber fruit is strange. It looks as though someone had stuck a bunch of green cucumbers on the stem of the tree, but they do ripen to a slightly red color. The fruit is a mixture of tart and sweetness, and though very tasty, we soon discovered, has powerful laxative properties. This caused the five of us to excuse ourselves on numerous occasions, the day after we first tried it. We renamed the fruit "squitter fruit."

The discovered lime and orange trees were suffocated by vines just like the guava were, so their fruit was also small and shriveled. Ken and Dave took the machete and spent an entire afternoon cutting them free of growth, clearing the area around them, and scraping the moss from their trunks. The difference this made was astounding, as some weeks later, they produced some decent fruit, though not an abundance.

This brings to mind the value of things on a deserted island, which one takes for granted in civilization. In this instance, toilet paper. Not to mention the toilet itself. We had been digging holes the first couple of days when we found an old long drop toilet. I am very familiar with these types of toilets, and I had learned from other places to place a lot of dried coconut husk down the bottom of the hole so as to prevent bad smells and flies. Don't ask me why or how it works, but it works very well. We repaired the box and seat, then fixed the structure around it to make a door for privacy.

So, back to the toilet paper. We were each rationed to a short piece of this luxury every day. One stifling hot morning, Ken carefully folded his precious piece of paper, tucked it into the elastic of his shorts, and then strode off to the toilet for a few minutes of privacy with one of his half-smoked rationed cigars. He had not been gone for very long when he returned with a most forlorn expression on his face that suggested his world had collapsed about him. When we asked him what the problem was, he answered that on his way to the toilet, a disaster had befallen him. The day was so hot and still that on his way, he had begun to perspire profusely, forgetting his precious paper resting against his skin, which by the time he got to the toilet, had been completely soaked by sweat. In evidence of this, he produced a soggy blob of paper for all of us to see. We did not budge. Leaves it had to be. It was, indeed, a sad day for him.

When it came to rationing, Ken believed that if we did not find diesel, we could be stranded on this island for a long time to come, - even a year or two, he reckoned, as it was unlikely anyone would come to such a remote place, either by plane or ship. So, we rationed everything we had left that had been rescued from the storm. We decided not to open any of the canned goods, as they would last longer, and I planned to make a charcoal cool box refrigerator to keep them cool.

For those interested, this is how it is made:

First, I would have to make charcoal from burning wood buried in soil (a major subsistence industry back in my home country, Zambia). Then I would construct a double-sided box-like structure using either wire or bamboo, making a space for the charcoal. The space would depend on the size of the structure—in my case, about a foot gap (except for the door to make that easier to open). Then the space is filled to make a "box" of charcoal, which then must be saturated with water at least twice a day. This gets absorbed into the charcoal. Wind and evaporation do the rest. This would even keep some of the fruit and fish fresh for a while.

We knew the perishable provisions (such as rice flour) would not last too long. The ladies were already removing the weevils from what was left of our rice and flour. Elisabeth and Nicole made a menu of what ration we would get on which day. Monday: oats porridge. Tuesday: cup of chocolate. Wednesday: two biscuits each, and so on.

We had personal stuff that needed rationing as well. For instance, we found that you really need very little toothpaste on your brush to clean your teeth. We rotated the toothpaste with sterile ash from the fire mixed to a paste with coconut water. Shampoo was not going to last long. We did have Colgate shampoo (which is the only shampoo that lathers in seawater), so we needed to use the soap sparingly. We were not heavy smokers, but all of us had to ration out our smokes to just two a day.

We had been on the island almost a week when Dave and I decided to do a reconnaissance deeper into the undergrowth. We cut our way through for an hour or so when Dave thought he saw something flash in the sun through the thicket. We cut our way through, and there on the ground was a stainless-steel, forty-five-gallon diesel drum!

Excitedly, Dave kicked it, but to our disappointment, it rang empty. Then we spotted another, then another. We ran to each drum, kicking them as we went, but the result was the same: all empty. We found another pile of containers farther on, and then made our way to them. We started kicking again, but each one rang empty. Dave and I started to swear in despair. Our initial excitement was now subdued as we just casually kicked one drum after another.

Suddenly, Dave shouted, "Hey, Gordon! Listen to this one."

As I approached, he kicked at a drum. It made a definite thump. No question, it was full! On that first scout, Dave and I found eleven full drums of diesel and one drum of petrol. We rushed back to the camp with the good news.

Ken was elated. He could now begin to work on his wooden tiller in earnest, and we could now get out of here and head for the Seychelles, and then onward to Kenya. He immediately planned how to get the diesel to the *Miken*.

I suddenly had mixed feelings about leaving this island. I was beginning to feel at home here.

Not long after we discovered the diesel, Elisabeth came to me and asked, "If the rest of them leave, can't we stay here?"

"I was thinking the exact same thing," I replied.

We did not notice Dave was close by, and he overheard us. "You know what," he said, "I was pumped to find the diesel, but now that I think about it - and between you and me - I'm never getting back on that boat again!"

We talked at length about what to do and how to approach Ken on the matter. I knew Ken wanted to get off the island, and Nicole didn't mind either way. I figured if Elisabeth and I stayed, Ken and Nicole could still make the journey to the Seychelles, but without Dave, it would make a tough and potentially dangerous voyage even more difficult. We would have to consider this very carefully before we made a decision. The decision was to be taken out of our hands.

The following day, Ken went to his boat to fire her up. After quite a while, he rowed back to camp and arrived with fury on his face. "The batteries are f—ing dead!" he said angrily and slumped into a chair, dejected.

Dave and I returned with Ken to the boat and checked all the batteries. They were definitely all flat with no life in them at all. Ken concluded that the alternator might be faulty. We decided to remove it and take it ashore to see if there was something we could do to repair it. Though at that stage, we didn't know what could be done.

So, unless we could find a way to get the batteries charged, we were now well and truly marooned on a deserted island, diesel or no diesel.

Extract from journal:

Thursday 1st January 1981

Gordon worked all day building a fowl run.
Nicole and I (Elisabeth) went in the bush looking for
squitter fruits. Found some but got badly bitten by
mosquitoes. Ken worked on boat. Stunning news,
batteries of the boat are flat. We have no way of
recharging them. Kenya is nearly 2000 miles away still
and we are stranded!

I cannot speak for the others, but for Elisabeth and I, this did bring about a different mindset. We began to consider the island our new home, at least for the foreseeable future. As if to confirm this, we discovered our house.

Taking a machete, Elisabeth and I went exploring inland. We hacked our way through thick growth for a couple of hours when quite suddenly I hit a wall. We cut and pulled the growth away from the wall to reveal a surprisingly large bungalow. Although the house was completely overgrown, it seemed in a very livable condition. For the rest of the day, I worked to clear as much away from the entrance and interior as I could. I managed to clear enough for Elisabeth and myself to move in that night. The following day, we worked on our hidden bungalow and its grounds in earnest.

A pathway cut through the jungle.

When one considers that the temperatures during the day reach above 43.5°C/110°F, it was surprising how motivated we were and how hard we worked to get our house cleared up. We chopped, hacked, pulled, and burned the trees and vines around the house until our hands were tender and blistered. After a few days of this, we also uncovered a well, close to which was a broken-down washroom and a stone throw from that was another "long drop" toilet.

I thoroughly cleared out the well until the water was fit enough for us to wash our clothes and water plants. We decided not to drink from this water unless we became desperate, and even then, we would boil and filter it. We did, however, use this water for the chickens, and they seemed to have no adverse effects drinking it.

The bungalow that Gordon and Elisabeth uncovered in the middle of the jungle, which became their home.

The pit toilet, including the seat, was in reasonably good repair and did not need much work to fix up. Behind the washhouse, I discovered a large steel water tank. With a lot of scrubbing, we soon had the tank clean. When this was done, I then built a guttering system below and along the length of the house's roof to the top of the water tank so as to collect any rainwater that ran from it. I found a short piece of pipe, which fit neatly into a hole at the base of the tank from inside the washroom. Then I plugged up the pipe's spout with a whittled piece of wood. Once tank is full of rainwater, stand underneath, remove plug and voilà! A freshwater shower.

The shower room uncovered at the bungalow.
Note: The water catchment Gordon built from the roof to the steel tank behind.

We were soon to get regular bursts of rain nearly every night for a while, so it was not long before the steel tank was full. This made our lives far more pleasant, as now we were able to enjoy a freshwater shower every day. We loved swimming in the sea but didn't particularly enjoy the sticky salt on our skin afterward, so it was great to be able to have a freshwater shower at the end of each day. But of course, the main benefit was to know we now had a good reservoir of drinking water at our disposal (at least as long as the rains kept coming). I collected one of the forty-five-gallon steel drums, and we cleaned it well and placed it next to the tank to catch any overflow. We used this water purely for drinking purposes.

In the grounds of the bungalow, we uncovered guava and orange trees. We freed them of the vines that smothered them, and then pruned any dead or dying branches. A few weeks later, the trees showed their appreciation and rewarded us with some much-welcomed fruit.

We had brought a badminton set with us, so I made a clearing behind the house for a court. This was to bring us many hours of fun.

From the big double-story house, we collected and carried two cupboards and a chest of drawers to our new home. The base for our bed had already been brought from the Clubhouse.

We now had an island home.

Later, we discovered another bungalow of the same design that had been burned down and was completely gutted.

Ken and Nicole made their place close to the lagoon, which was a lot more comfortable, and moved in.

Dave was still looking for a place for himself. The store shed was too big and open, and he did not fancy the jailhouse. There did not seem to be much else.

Eventually, Dave did find a lonely hut on the ocean side of the island. There was nothing else around it, so why it was there was somewhat of a mystery. Perhaps in the past it had been used as a lookout post. Dave cleaned it up and moved in.

No matter what any of us were doing during the day, most evenings we would get together at the Clubhouse, enjoy a meal together, play board games or cards, and just relax. Ken had a radio that could pick up BBC World Service. To save the batteries, we would only listen for an hour each night. It was good to hear some music and connected us to the outside world, even if only for a short while. There were a couple of nights where the radio started to ping over and over, very similar to the sonar sound I have heard on World War II submarine movies. We found that strange. Even stranger still, on a very calm night, we heard an eerie sound that had us all stop and listen. It sounded like a young child crying. We tried to hear where it was coming from when the sobbing suddenly stopped. We all looked at each other, then brushed it off as being a bird or some wildlife. Aside from the various types of birds, the only animals on the island we knew of were a few rats. We would hear that strange sound again.

The following morning, Nicole and Elisabeth decided to experiment with the food resources the island offered. The first and most obvious was the coconut palm and its fruit, which is extremely versatile. To begin with, there is the cool, fresh, sweet water of the green nut and the soft jelly inside of it. Then there is the mature nut that can be grated, soaked in water, then squeezed in a cloth, which results in coconut milk. We used this milk when making rice pudding, chapattis, and bread. To make coconut oil, I would pack the grated coconut into one of my long socks to use as a sieve, then pour hot water into it and run it into a bowl. I would then place this in the charcoal cooler and leave it there until it congealed. (If this did not work, then I would just hang it in a bag until it separated.) The liquid part I would discard then boil the rest over the fire, watching it carefully so it didn't burn until it separated further. With this process, from three mature coconuts, I could make a small cup of coconut oil. Coconut flour can also be made from this, but we never got around to doing that.

One can also make coconut sweets by simply cutting the mature nut into strips and heating in a pan over the fire, which turns into coconut caramel. A favorite treat all of us enjoyed.

Another favorite was looking for coconuts that had just begun to shoot. They look almost rotten, and the nut inside turns soft and swells to fill the entire shell. We ate this as dessert after a meal. It is slightly salty but also very sweet and soft. Elisabeth called it coconut marshmallow.

My favorite was palm heart (known as millionaire salad). This was harvested from young palms that still had green stems. We cut down these stems and laid them on a table. Then the outer part peeled open to reveal in the center a Swiss roll of the finest salad in the world. I know this can be bought in cans, but as it is preserved in brine, it is absolutely nothing like the real fresh palm heart.

The finest salad in the world – Palm heart.

Jaggery, or palm sugar, is also obtained from the palm. This is done by climbing up to the spadix, or flower, and slicing the petals or the green soft part below. The sap that runs out is caught in a container and collected. (The limes we found came in handy for this, as wiping the lime juice in the catch container prevents fermentation.) This sap is then boiled and crystallized, and voilà! You have sugar. The sap, in turn, can be fermented to make toddy, otherwise known as palm wine. Arrack alcohol can be made from this as well. I prefer to make toddy another way:

take three green coconuts, pour the water out into a bowl, add a tablespoon of sugar and yeast (we had some yeast), sieve into a bottle, cover with cloth to breathe, place in a cool spot (charcoal cooler), and you have palm wine twenty-four hours later. This can also be distilled to make the moonshine arrack.

Gordon collecting jaggery syrup from the spadix of the coconut palm.

Ken did find a thin tube that made a perfect fit to a pressure cooker he had, which then doubled up as a still, so we could have a small sundowner every now and then. So, here's to island living, cheers!

Then, of course, the tree itself and its palms have many practical uses as well. According to a Chinese saying, there are as many useful properties in the palm tree as there are days in the year. My favorite story on the coconut palm, however, is a legend I heard in Sri Lanka, where a man once was tasked to find a gift worthy of the gods. After traveling the world for many years, he returned to his home, went into his backyard, and picked a king coconut.

We were also blessed with a fair supply of breadfruit. Roasted on fire coals, this fruit tasted not unlike roasted chestnut. Boiled and mashed, it is very similar to mashed potatoes. When sliced and fried, it makes delicious chips. If the breadfruit is left to ripen, it turns soft and yellow, becoming pulpy, which, when eaten raw, is similar to sweet avocado pear. Elisabeth and Nicole made a small supply of jam from this fruit as well.

The vines produced a bean that gave us our vegetable diet.

We found some berries, but the birds did not seem to eat them, so before we tried them, we caught a rat and fed it some of the berries. When the rat would not eat them either, we left them alone.

Watching what the birds eat, though, nearly caught me out. I was exploring a new part of the island on my own when I spotted a tree full of yellow fruit. A large flock of snow-white fairy terns were feasting on them, which I found surprising, because as far as I knew, these birds only ate seafood. I picked one of the fruits and put it to my tongue. It was acidic but sweet and tasted good, so I climbed to pick as much as I could to carry back to camp, eating a few as I went. The fairy terns were not happy with me being in their tree and constantly dive-bombed me. I arrived at the Clubhouse and shared my find with everyone.

While in Sri Lanka, Dave had picked up a free pamphlet in a pharmacy that showed a few tropical trees. He took one of the fruits and tried to identify it from the booklet.

"Stop eating!" he shouted at us. "Gordon, is this the tree?" He pointed at a picture of a tree with a sample of the fruit in a square box below it.

No question, that was it. The heading above the picture read, "strychnine tree!" It turned out that though the flesh of the fruit was edible, the seeds of the fruit were highly toxic. I reckoned I had spat out all the seeds I had eaten, but I wasn't entirely sure. It was a long night for me. Thankfully, I awoke in the morning none the worse.

Elisabeth and I decided to take a break from the work and go shelling in the lagoon. It was a hot and serenely calm day, so we rowed out in the dinghy together to the deeper water on the reef.

Elisabeth diving for shells.

Some shells, especially old ones, are easy to spot, but most are not. They camouflage quite well, and if you do not know what to look for, it's easy to miss them. Following trails is always a good giveaway for those buried in the sand. I dove a few tiger cowries, looking for their brightly colored dresses that gives them away. I also dove some beautiful five-finger conches and textile cones. (The latter have to be handled with great care, as they can dart an unwary hand with a deadly toxin.) The shells I dove, I passed on to Elisabeth, who was above me in the dinghy. As Elisabeth is an amateur conchologist, she wanted to try her luck snorkeling in the shallows. She did not have much success at first so on our return to the beach, she decided to gather many different types of smaller shells that were littered everywhere on the shoreline.

She returned with a multitude of various small shells and proudly placed them neatly on the white sandy floor of the Clubhouse for us all to appreciate. A short while later, we heard Elisabeth laughing out loud at her own folly. We all went to see what the hilarity was all about. There, Elisabeth stood with her hands on her hips and faking a pouting lip. We all looked down to see small tracks across the sand in all directions. All of us cracked up laughing hysterically as we watched half her shell collection scurry away as the resident hermit crabs inside them took off!

At breakfast the following morning, Ken announced he would look around to find material to construct a windmill. This would then be used in conjunction with the recovered alternator (which he hoped to service) from the boat's engine and hopefully use it to charge the dead batteries. If that worked, he would then begin work on the planned wooden hand-controlled tiller rudder.

Nicole decided she wanted to take a walk on her own and see what she could discover, while Elisabeth went to collect wild beans.

Dave and I had already planned to go check out a part of the island we had not been to yet. After some time of cutting through thick growth, we came into a large clearing, and there in the center was a small, beautiful church built of stone (which must have been brought from the mainland).

We went inside to find four twin rows of wooden pews, still in surprisingly good condition. There was a small altar, on which stood a statue of St. Joseph, beside which lay a broken-down figurine of St. Mary.

The church was surprisingly cool inside (we would later come here if we wanted a respite from the heat or just to have some quiet time). Another pleasant thing about this church was that there were never any flies or mosquitoes inside, ever.

Dave took some of the pews and used them to build a cot-type bed for his small house on the other side of the island.

We returned midday to join Elisabeth and Ken at the Clubhouse, and we all grabbed a bite to eat. Nicole had not yet returned.

Sometime late that afternoon, we were beginning to wonder why Nicole had been away for so long. Toward evening, I decided to track her down. Just before dark, I heard her calling and found her. She said she was terribly lost. Now, you may think this would be difficult to do on such a small island, but when surrounded by such thick vegetation, inexperienced people can quickly become disorientated.

Elisabeth and I went off the next day to the southern part of the island, and to our surprise, found it was quite different to the heavy growth of the northern side. Here, it was almost like a park of open grassland and casuarinas trees. There was even a small, brackish marsh. In the days to come, Elisabeth and I would come here for some alone time and just lay in the shade of our pine forest and listen to the waves. Some days, Elisabeth would even manage to rustle up a makeshift picnic basket. On the way back, we found some large breadfruit trees, which I decided to climb up to collect fruit for the camp. Multitudes of mosquitoes were feeding on the sap of the breadfruit and had apparently been waiting for a half-naked body such as mine for years, so I soon became an unwilling blood donor. I scurried to the top of the tree and grabbed a couple of melon-sized breadfruit, then got the hell out of there. From then on, whenever we went breadfruit climbing, we would dress up fit for Sunday school to protect ourselves as best we could from the mosquitoes and their built-in syringes.

Dressed up against the mosquitos while exploring the jungle in search of breadfruit.

Flies were becoming a major pest as well, especially during meals. When we first arrived on the island, we would wash out our plates, pots, and pans in the jungle close by, where the crabs would clean up any leftovers. The unconsidered consequence of this was an invasion of flies.

This became an annoyance for all of us, but one day it did give us a laugh at Ken's expense one day. He was infinitely irritated by them, and so, of course, they seemed to pick on him more than the rest of us. After lunch on this particular day, he decided to head for the lagoon to escape them. He soon came storming back, shouting several expletives as the flies followed him.

Ken took one of his half-smoked cigars, put a hat on his head, and headed back toward the lagoon. The rest of us sat in the Clubhouse, and with a clear view, watched in amusement as Ken strode into the shallows of the lagoon, where he sat down with just his head out of the water, his cigar smoke puffing out his mouth like a steam train, cursing profusely as a swarm of flies still buzzed around his head.

We did eventually manage to significantly diminish this annoyance by building proper soakaways for dirty dishwater. We did this using old drums, which we had cut off the tops and bottoms, buried them most of the way into the ground, then made a cover for the end sticking out above ground.

We also made a "twenty-four-hour pot." Our large cast-iron pot was kept on the fire, and any decent leftovers - fish, turtle, shellfish, clam, even beans - was put in the pot. As long as this was brought to a boil every twenty-four hours, it would never spoil, and in fact, become tastier as time went on. It was always close to the fire, so it was handy for whenever we needed a quick bite to eat.

Any unusable leftovers such as fish bones were either buried far from the Clubhouse or collected and dropped out at sea. I also discovered some citronella grass. I found that if I chewed on a stem after a meal, this would not only refresh the mouth but also keep the flies away. Also, if the citronella was boiled with some coconut oil and sieved through one of my socks, the resulting ointment could be used as a mosquito repellent for when we went to collect breadfruit. (Strangely, these mosquitoes were daytime pests, never at night as I was used to elsewhere.)

On the subject of citronella, Elisabeth would take some the leaves of this lemongrass and make a refreshing tea or drink.

On the evening of the thirty-first of December, we all dressed up in our "finest clothes," such as they were, and gathered at the Clubhouse to celebrate the arrival of the New Year. The evenings we spent at the club were blissfully free of flies and mosquitoes.

That night, as were most, was calm and peaceful. The area in front of the shed had been cleared, so we had a lovely moonlit view of the lagoon and the beach. The stars were reflecting like sparkles on the surface of the calm water, only disturbed every now and then as a fish dashed through the fluorescence in the sea. Our fire, glowing brightly, displayed dancing shadows on the vines and trees surrounding us while we relaxed in the light of a gently hissing hurricane lamp, accompanied by the BBC World Service playing some pleasant background music.

Our supper was a treat of canned steak and kidney pudding, especially saved for the occasion, followed by a precious tin of canned fruit. After this fine meal, we opened our only bottle of brandy I had been keeping. Ken offered his precious few cigars, and we sat back in our cane chairs and celebrated in style the coming and arrival of the New Year:1981.

This did bring to mind how our family and friends might be celebrating the New Year, and we could not help thinking how worried they might be should they not hear from us soon. Ken reckoned we could be stranded on the island for a couple of years before anyone would discover us and a rescue would come, in which case our families would expect the worst - that is, that we had all been lost at sea.

We decided from that night on that our rationing would be even more stringent and that most of our food would have to come from the sea, supplemented by what we could gather from the island. The last of our rice and flour was tied up to the beams to keep them from the rats. Any other food was kept off the floor, safe from crabs, and all our tables and cupboard legs were placed in bowls of water to keep ants from the food (ironically, we had a couple of mice use the bowls for drinking).

We also had to consider injuries now. When one knows there is a reachable medical facility, one tends to take more risks. Out here, though, in the middle of the Indian Ocean, a serious injury could be a death sentence, as in all tropical areas. Even small injuries could become severely infected and gangrenous.

Ken kept voicing his concerns about the sharks I had to deal with on an almost daily basis, or even a fall from one of the breadfruit trees that could spell disaster. We had to weigh our risks carefully from now on. Fortunately, in this regard, the injury to Ken's foot finally began to heal.

It wasn't long, though, before we all started to develop tropical sores on our legs. Strangely, a decent cut would heal well, but a small nick or scratch would get infected quickly, growing into a small boil. No amount of antiseptic would help heal them, and the flies would constantly be at them. With few bandages left, we had to resort to wearing long socks that Elisabeth had stitched together to use as bandages to keep the flies off. After a while, we got used to the sores and even gave them names, checking every morning to see if "Charlie" was worse than "Freddy," and so on. Eventually, we were to find out that just soaking our legs for twenty minutes each day in soapy freshwater would heal the tropical sores in little to no time, better than any ointment we had.

Our wind turbine Mark Five

While Dave, Elisabeth, and I were working on our respective houses, Ken designed and built windmills to attach to the alternator as wind chargers, to see if he could generate enough spin to charge up the batteries. Mark One spun in the wind pretty well but did not produce any charge. Ken kept on making windmills right up to Mark Five, the last one spinning so furiously that I figured we might even use it to fly out of here. But it still would not produce any charge. The alternator had to be faulty beyond our means to repair. Ken was beginning to get seriously frustrated.

Up to this point, we had all been getting on extremely well, but for a brief period after this, the mood changed.

As pointed out before, there is no question that Ken was the skipper on the boat, and that is as it should be. On the island, however, I valued as much independence Elisabeth and I could have under the circumstances. All meals were a communal affair with all of us pitching in, but for the rest, we began to do our own thing, helping each other because we wanted to, not because we had to. It was not uncommon for Ken to thank me for the food I provided from the sea. Most of the breadfruit tree and palm climbing for jaggery was done by Elisabeth and myself, all the makings from the coconut, water collection, salt making, and much else we did because we enjoyed doing it, not because we felt obliged to. Ken seemed to understand this and left me to do what I do, asking for help when he needed it like any good neighbor would do, and I afforded him the same. However, Ken did rope in Dave for any project he wanted to tackle, and right now it was to help him build the tiller rudder.

While they worked together on the rudder, the classic school-playground affliction of "us against them" began to manifest itself, and my initial concern at the beginning of our voyage about Dave being the odd one out started to play out to some degree. Elisabeth is one of those people who gets on with everybody but can be aggressive if she perceives she or I are under attack. She brought to my attention that she had overheard some things said by Dave and Nicole. It was not unexpected, but I found it sad, silly, totally counterproductive, and unnecessary. I knew I had to nip it in the bud before we slipped into a mini *Lord of the Flies* scenario.

Later, I noticed Dave walking out alone to the end of the broken-down jetty, so I saw my chance and joined him there. I did not beat about the bush and asked him outright if what Elisabeth had overheard was true. Dave then began to say a few things about Ken and Nicole. I pointed out to him that, from the outset, I had warned about this happening. That is, if he did not have a partner on the venture, he might feel the need to bond with someone at the expense of the others. I told him I would not be party to joining any sides against anyone but considered him a good friend, as I did the others. It would be a real shame to spoil this incredible adventure all of us were on together. I went on to say that I knew it could slide even further if tensions and frustrations grew as time went on, resulting in not only some useless unpleasantness but danger.

Dave thought about it for a moment and agreed we should guard against any of that creeping in between us. Dave and I then enjoyed the rest of the day in each other's company, and I made a mental note to speak to Elisabeth about making sure Dave never felt left out.

Later that night, we all gathered at the Clubhouse, where I pulled Ken aside and confronted him about the issue. He assured me this had nothing to do with him, as it was not his style. He did say, however, that Nicole considered herself a Parisian feminist (whatever that means) who took some issue with me being "macho."

We all then sat together to have a meal, and I asked Nicole what her beef was with me. She said she did not think it was fair that she, Elisabeth, and even Dave collected beans and I never did.

Before I could respond, Elisabeth got up and grabbed my speargun and diving gear, walked over to Nicole, and calmly placed them at her feet. "I will pick Gordon's share of beans tomorrow, Nicole, while you take the speargun and go face the sharks to get food to feed us."

Needless to say, I was never asked to pick beans again.

The island and nature of our situation was defining our roles, far removed from the concrete jungle of Paris. For a couple of days after this, there was a level of discomfort between us, but it did not last long, and a sense of understanding and acceptance of each other's talents and contributions connected us more than divided us. And importantly, our independence was respected. There were, of course, to be other disagreements to come, but they were few. I am sure if asked, the others would all have their own take on this, which may differ from mine.

Elisabeth and I took a walk together on the far-side beach to be alone for a while, when we chanced upon some strange footprints in the sand. They had been distorted by the rising water, so it was difficult to identify them and had us perplexed and intrigued. What the hell had made them?

We had to return to camp, so I decided I would return later and track down whatever it was. However, before I could do so, that very night, we were to dramatically find out exactly what it was.

Later that night when Elisabeth and I retired to our bungalow in the middle of the jungle, the full moon lit up the island, almost clear as day.

I had slashed a pathway to the house, which made a tunnel of undergrowth. On the way there, we once again heard the strange sound of a small child sobbing but could not see beyond the jungle tunnel to see what it was.

Elisabeth said it was "really creeping her out" and wanted to get to the house quickly. We arrived at the bungalow, left the doors open to our bedroom for the breeze, and climbed into bed. Just as we got comfortable, we heard the sobbing sound again just outside of the open door to the veranda.

I climbed quietly out of the bed and slowly made my way to the patio outside, afraid of what I might find there. The floor creaked beneath my feet and the sound stopped. I searched all around outside the house. There was nothing to be seen.

Later, a little after midnight, something woke Elisabeth up. She reached over gently and shook me awake, whispering that there was someone, or something, in the room.

143

I sat up slowly and looked about the moonlit room. I could see nothing unusual. The only sound was that of the wind in the palm trees. What I did notice, however, was an unfamiliar musky smell in the room. Though the moonlight did light up the room, it also cast a dark shadow in the corner that I could not see into.

I stared into this black patch when two huge nostrils appeared out of it, followed by an enormous elongated face with long, droopy ears hanging down either side of the monstrous face. It gradually revealed itself out of the darkness of the corner.

Elisabeth screamed an ear-piercing screech. The poor donkey honked in equal terror, and in blind panic, ran straight into the wall. Half dazed, it turned and ran straight into the opposite wall, honking in unison with Elisabeth's hysterical screams as though they were trying to outdo each other. More by chance than good judgment, the beast charged through the door to the adjoining room and disappeared over the veranda, honking in terror as he went.

Our nighttime 'monster'
Note: Badminton court cleared in the backyard with the well and long drop toilet in the background.

We discovered later there were eleven wild donkeys on the island.

We never did find what caused the sounds of a child sobbing, but later, I heard about a tourist who had been left stranded on an island in the Seychelles. A week later, when it was realized by the tour operators that he had been left behind, they returned to find the man (who obviously must have had no survival skills) on death's door, and they had to Helivac him out on a stretcher with a saline drip. Interestingly, in a later interview, he also spoke of hearing the strange sound of a child crying.

Growing up in the African Bush, I have become a reasonably good tracker; however, I could not find any tracks that would help identify the culprit. I can only assume the stranded tourist did not hear the same ghost we did. It must have been some kind of bird.

One of the other fascinating creatures on the island was the great coconut crab. They look the same as the ordinary hermit crab but much larger—so much so that no seashell is big enough to house them, so they take over coconut shells instead. Then there are the fellows that reach a size where even a coconut is too small for them and carry no house at all. These monsters are either bright red and orange, or purple, and can grow over a foot and a half long. They are also the only crabs known to climb trees, which they do in order to pluck coconut from the palms. Their pincers are so powerful they have no trouble opening a coconut. Apparently, when Charles Darwin placed one of these crabs in a strong tin box, the creature actually cut its way out.

The giant coconut crab is known to be good eating, but as there were not many on the island, we let them be. They were also quite fearless. Often when we walked through the jungle and came across one, they would stand their ground by stomping their feet and challenging us with their huge pincers.

The coconut-toting crabs often amused us when they visited at night in the Clubhouse. They would immediately hijack any mug or can left on the ground, discard their grubby old coconuts, move into their spanking new home, and attempt to sneak off into the jungle with their new house. It was a strange sight to see a coffee mug, or a "Made in Hong Kong" tin can waddle off into the undergrowth before we went to arrest them.

We also used these coconut crabs to stage a derby. We would catch several, draw different numbers on their coconut shells with coral chalk, and then place them underneath a large bowl on the white sand. We then would draw a larger circle of about a five-foot radius around the bowl. Each person then would place their bet on whichever crab they fancied. The stakes could be pretty high, as much as a whole cigarette! We then would lift the bowl—and they were off! Well, not quite. Some would just remain where they were and go to sleep. Others would gradually move away, building up speed as they went. The first crab to reach the outer circle was the winner. Of course, the crabs would respond to a lot of enthusiastic cheering, especially should you see a crab that was not yours ahead of the race. This would be sure to make him duck into their shell and stop before the line, which would give your crab a chance to catch up. But then it also backfired if your crab ducked instead just as he was about to win, which happened frustratingly often, then turn and go the other way, or walk in a circle right along the winning line, round and round, almost as if he were purposely doing this to annoy you. Still, it brought us hours of fun.

The Clubhouse also became our gaming place. We had Scrabble, chess, and mastermind board games. We also pooled all our books in the small library Nicole had made, so we could just relax and enjoy a good read.

We would also sit and solve all the problems of the world here in the evenings, with varying discussions. The night after we told the others about the donkey, we once again heard the sobbing child in the jungle, and the discussion turned to paranormal topics. That night, it was quite late when Dave decided to head for his little hut way across the other side of the island.

This is what he told us the following morning:

The discussion of the paranormal and the eerie sobbing already had him "spooked" when he headed for his hut. As he walked the path, he felt the jungle closing in on him. On the way, he dodged giant coconut crabs that snapped at his feet and passed by the old wooden mansion, which silhouetted in the moonlight. Its creaking window shutters reminded him of something out of an Alfred Hitchcock horror movie. Dave hastened his pace, as he now heard something moving around him. He quickened his step, finally reaching his isolated hut, clambered into his cot, and eventually went to sleep.

Dave said he awoke late in the night, horrified to find something in his cot with him. It was gently touching and stroking his face. He gingerly felt to see what it was and discovered something long and hairy alongside his face and extending above his head. Dave swore and brushed it away, but it would not go. Shouting, he grabbed at it to chuck it out of the cot, but it just came back at him. Screaming in terror, he punched frantically at it, desperately trying to get it out of his cot with no luck. Fortunately, before he actually killed it, the circulation in his battered "dead" arm returned, and Dave came to the realization that he was beating on his own arm that had drained and gone to "sleep," crooked above his head. It was his own fingers that had been touching his face.

We were all doubled over in laughter as Dave told his sorry tale, still nursing a tender arm.

Dave had been showing some interest in learning how to spearfish and free dive. In turn, he said he would teach me how to surf, which is one water sport I had never really gotten the hang of. So, I asked him if he was up to joining me on a dive to the outer reef, and he said he was.

Before we went, I told him that we would be spearing fish, so the sharks *would* come, no question, and that buddy diving with sharks is always better than solo. If an aggressive shark appears, buddy divers can go back-to-back and appear bigger to the shark, but mostly they can watch each other's backs. I also advised him to keep away from waves breaking on the reef, as it causes bad visibility there, and to always keep the sharks in view. It is also important to watch if a shark arches its back and drops its pectoral fins. This is usually a sign it is coming in, and if it does, then one must act aggressively toward it. A poke it on its very sensitive snout will usually make it turn away.

The sea was calm and clear while the sun shone brightly - perfect conditions, which promised a pleasant dive. While swimming out among the corals, we spotted two large, fat lobsters. I managed to catch one of them, of which Dave took charge. Swimming farther out, I caught sight of two smaller lobsters, both of which I captured. As I had no fish buoy with me on this dive, I would thread smaller fish through the spear onto my line. Soon a small, red snapper fish and a small rock cod were hanging on the line of the spear gun.

Eventually, we came to the edge of the coral table and deep, blue sea. I searched the drop-off here and spotted a good-sized grouper coming out his cave, surely on his way to catch his dinner. Dave and I stalked the fish for a while, then I dove after him. When I was within range, I fired. My line extended about fifteen feet and the small fish I had strung on the line were hanging three-quarters of the way from the spear. My aim was true, and the spear found its mark. Without warning, a lemon shark shot out from the deep, blue water at high speed and snatched my catch on the line, not three feet in front of me.

My first thought was *My spear!* If the grouper swam off with it, the most certain way of getting food would be lost. Fortunately, I had hit the grouper a "kill shot," and the fish had died almost instantly but was slowly sinking into the deep with my spear in it.

I took a deep breath and dove after the grouper to retrieve both the fish and, more importantly, the spear. I reached the grouper at about forty feet, which was okay going down, but going up with such a big fish made me bless the jet fins I was using. To make matters worse, the lemon shark was circling above me, obviously now believing I was to supply him with a main course.

I was not about to give up my big catch. When I hit the surface, I thrusted the spear through the grouper which I used to fend the shark off. The lemon shark followed us all the way into the shallows, but he never took my fish from me.

Dave had handled his first encounter with an aggressive shark very well, but when we got back to camp, he turned to me and said conclusively, "Guess I will leave the spear fishing to you!"

But it was not to be his last attempt.

The following day, I planned an expedition to reach one of the islands alongside ours. On the low spring tide, it was possible to wade across a great deal of the way to the two adjacent islands. Elisabeth and Nicole asked to come along. When the tide was at its lowest, we headed out. We were about halfway across the coral reef that separated the islands when I spotted a curious phenomenon.

At first, I thought it was a huge octopus, its arms waving above the water like a Medusa. But closer inspection disproved this theory, as this animal had twice as many arms as any common eight-armed octopus I was familiar with, and the massive arms were a greenish yellow. Excited that I might have discovered a new species of sea creature, I cautiously moved closer to the waving mass, hoping to get a better look. When I was a couple of feet away, the creature disintegrated and broke into pieces, each arm swimming off in a different direction. For a moment, I stared in fascinated disbelief before I realized the "arms" were, in fact, large moray eels all feeding on an octopus in a hole just big enough to accommodate all their heads. This gave the illusion of a large, single creature with many arms.

The moray eel is armed with a vicious set of teeth, and can be very aggressive, especially when provoked. So, while some of these came straight at me, I made a hasty retreat. I had not gotten far when a pain sliced across the underside of my foot, and the water around me turned a bloody red.

Nicole and Elisabeth helped me back to shore, where upon inspection there showed a nasty coral cut right along the length of my foot.

The laceration underneath my foot kept me out of the sea for nearly a week. Fortunately, the grouper I had speared the day before would last us for two days. (Fish kept for a day when cooked.) I still had to find alternative means to catch fish until the wound healed.

That night, Dave said if I took the dinghy out on the reef, where he could make a quick exit out the water, he would try to spear a fish himself. I said that sounded like a good plan.

The next day (accompanied by Elisabeth), we rowed out to the reef. Before Dave went into the water, I advised him not to spear a parrotfish, even though it was tempting to do so. They were plentiful, and some were very large; however, they had tough, leathery skin, and the spear would often not penetrate deep enough. (Also, inexperienced spear fishermen don't often realize that, due to refraction, the target is actually farther away than it looks). So, these fish are easily wounded, and should that happen, its flapping around underwater would be a dinner bell to all the sharks in the area. Anyway, to my taste, parrotfish is also not very good eating.

Dave slipped off the dinghy into the water while Elisabeth and I waited. Dave did not want to settle for a small fish, but we could see he struggled to get a big one. After quite a while, he moved away from the dinghy, closer to the edge of the reef, where the larger fish were more often found. There, we watched as he duck-dived, obviously after something. When he surfaced, he was looking face down into the water, sweeping his head from side to side. The next thing he did was flip back to us like crazy at full speed, his flippers pounding like an outboard engine. Even from where we were, we could see the sharks coming in.

He cleared the water into the dinghy in one frantic movement, declaring, "That's it, I'm done!"

"You nailed a parrot fish?" I asked.

"Couldn't resist," he confirmed.

So, I decided I would try hand line fishing until my foot healed. The end of the old, broken-down jetty seemed the best place to give this a try, and it was only for a short time. Small fish, varied and plentiful, were easily caught. Larger fish were trevally (surely for its size on of the greatest game fish in the world), rock cod, snapper, jackfish, rays, moray eel, Longtom, grouper, nurse and blacktip sharks, and last but not least, the famous game fish that was so eulogized by Zane Grey: the bonefish.

However, other than sharks, the larger fish were few here off the old jetty. Sharks were numerous, and a staple part of our diet. Contrary to popular thought, we found sharks were good to eat, and it was a pleasure to sink one's teeth into a generous chunk of meat without any worry of fish bones.

Back from a successful dive.
Note: The Miken moored in the distance, the broken-down old jetty and the dinghy moored in the shallows.

When the fishing was slow on the jetty, we would row out to the edge of the coral and fish from there. On the opposite side of the island, a great deal of coral was bared at low tide. Here armed with a wooden spear I had fashioned I would catch octopus and moray eel, both of which we considered delicacies. Elisabeth liked to join me in the shallows of the exposed corals to hunt for moray eels. Here, we would lift loose coral heads to find them. As they darted around our ankles, we would attempt to spear or hit them. For some reason, the morays always darted away from me but invariably straight towards Elisabeth, where, instead of hitting them, she would prance away, shrieking as she went splashing away. Undeterred, she would still keep trying, always with the same result. This soon became known as Elisabeth's moray jig!

Moray eel delicacy.
Note: Clubhouse in the background
Also, note the socks sewn together as bandages.

On one of these hunts, Elisabeth discovered a coral garden with a host of tiger cowries. She collected some for our collection.

Although I did enjoy the fishing, it was also a vital part of our survival. Ken was concerned that if I could not dive for some reason, they would need a way to catch fish themselves. So, he set about preparing a fishnet he had stowed among his equipment.

That evening, he and Dave rowed out to the edge of the coral and set it up. The following day, they rowed out again to see what the net had caught and returned, disappointed. Sharks had torn great holes in the net and rendered it useless.

Undeterred, Ken found some old chicken wire and constructed a fish trap. When complete, we placed the trap beside the jetty along with a good supply of crushed sea urchin as bait. The trap was more successful than the net and supplied us with a few small fish.

The fish trap gave me the idea of constructing a lobster pot. However, this proved unsuccessful. I had more success diving for these tasty crustaceans.

One of the tasks I took responsibility for was taking care of the chickens. I noticed there were some maize seeds in the feed we had brought for them. As it happened, Dave was studying horticulture, so I pointed this out to him. Then he and I tried our luck at planting them. It did not take long before the maize started to grow. My patch looked a bit sad, but Daves' garden flourished and grew as if time itself was against them. Dave also collected some young banana shoots and planted a mini plantation of them.

The chickens were now almost fully grown, and we all anxiously awaited our first egg. You may remember that when we were in Galle, we had asked a local gentleman to bring us one male chicken and four lady chickens. Well, it turns out - yup, they grew into four male chickens and one very happy lady chicken!

Extract from journal:

Monday 12 January 1981.

Porridge day! Everyone is up early so as to not miss out on the porridge as Monday is the only day we're allowed it. It is also my birthday (Elisabeth). Gordon has a birthday surprise for me, our only hen has laid her first egg. Gordon swam to his lobster pot hoping for a lobster for my birthday lunch. His pot has been destroyed by the rough seas last night. He did find me a lovely pearl oyster though. Everyone told me not to do anything so I really felt lazy. It has been raining a lot. I had the last bit of brandy as I am feeling bad with a sore throat

The next day, we had a heavy rainstorm, so Elisabeth, saying she was not feeling well, stayed in bed the whole day. That afternoon, she began to run a high temperature and her fever reached its pitch that night. I battled to get her fever down as best I could with damp towels, the outside heat and humidity conspiring against her.

I was seriously getting concerned when her fever finally broke with the rising of the early-morning sun. Elisabeth sat up, feeling groggy, but asked for some water. She stayed in bed for the rest of the day and, though still a bit weak, managed to get out of bed the following day. The cause of the fever is still a mystery; we have no idea what brought it on. This, once again, brought discussion of what we would do if one of us got injured or became seriously ill.

This was of particular concern to Ken, who said he was now feeling more and more responsible for our wellbeing, and after Elisabeth's bout with fever, repeatedly asked "Gordon, what if Elisabeth's fever did not break or what if you get you get bitten by a shark?"

As much as Elisabeth and I loved the island, it was becoming obvious that Ken was aching to get off.

In order to give my usual dive haunts a rest, I went spearfishing off some coral on the far side of the island, which I had wanted to try for some time. Here under swallow water, a coral table stretched more than a mile out to sea, then ended abruptly in a sheer drop that disappeared into deep, blue water.

I swam out to the drop-off to look for bigger game fish, and without pausing in the shallow water, I swam directly out to the deep. As I cleared the edge, I saw beneath me a splendor that few places in the world could equal. The light green of the shallow water changed gradually to a turquoise, then a light blue, and finally became the rich, deep blue of the Indian Ocean. Below me, the corals were stunningly beautiful with a multitude of different species of coral fishes.

I was so enraptured by the sight below me that, without thinking, I swam over the edge with the intention of swimming along the coral cliff. As I left the shallow water and entered the deep blue, I unexpectedly found myself in the grip of a powerful current that took hold of me and forcefully dragged me out to sea. The endless space of the deep now took on a menacing feel, as I had a fairly good idea what the shark population out there must be like.

The normal procedure when caught in strong currents is to try and swim with the flow instead of exhausting yourself by going against it, until you find a place the current will allow you to come in. This is fine if you are on a coastline, but it does not work on an island; you will just be dragged out to open sea.

So, on this occasion, I battled it. I tried to call for help, but no one was within earshot. My jet fins were powerful, but I could not make headway back to the coral shelf. I was beginning to tire, when I spotted a large coral head farther to my left, protruding off the reef's drop-off. It was quite far out, about the same distance that I was from the cliff face. I edged sideways toward it, flipping madly to maintain the same distance, when, eventually, I came up to the coral head. I kicked with all my might and desperately grabbed for the coral. But I was still just out of reach, no matter how much I pumped my fins. The current pulled me farther away when, in sheer exasperation, I shot into the coral head with my spear gun, and miraculously, the spear took hold. The current swung me closer to the reef, but I could still not quite reach the edge, but with this purchase, I managed to ease myself to the coral, praying with each slow overhand, the spear would not come loose. Eventually, I reached the coral head, hugging it for a moment, then pulled myself over and collapsed, exhausted, in the shallow coral table.

I had hardly caught my breath when a nosey nurse shark, about four feet long, came bearing down on me. I was in no mood to be sociable. I scrambled to load my speargun, shot him at close range, stood up in the water, and dragged him till I could grab his tail. The shark tried his best to turn on me, but we danced all the way to the shore, where I dispatched him for supper. The nurse shark was our favorite shark to eat.

When the shark was safely landed, I went out again to look for lobster. I found a beauty tucked beneath a coral head, under which I also found a five-finger seashell. I decided to search around a bit longer, and within a short period, I had a collection of several cowries, some conches and six-finger shells. This area became our most regular "shelling" spot. After some time, Elisabeth and I had amassed a good collection of shells, whereas the others in the group had only a handful.

So, Ken approached me and said, "I know we agreed that everyone would collect their own shells, but I think we should pool what we find and share them."

I laughed and said I had no problem with that, as long as everybody helped clean them. Ken agreed that was fair.

However, cleaning shells is not a pleasant affair. The meat of them cannot be removed completely without damaging the shell (except the helmet shell, which, when slammed on its knuckle side into the sand, will come out whole, the meat of which makes a fine steak). Other shells, however, needed to be buried and left for a week or so then collected and taken into the shallow water where we would smack the shells face down into the water to dislodge the rotten meat inside. The smell is indescribably foul.

The first time we all went down to clean the shells, everybody was gung-ho and keen. After that session, the others bailed on any further shell cleaning, and it was left to Elisabeth and myself. The shells were still to be shared though.

Our only hen was now laying an egg a day. We oiled these to prevent them from turning bad, and we all had an egg treat every five days. Cocky became protective of his territory, and although he and I were still pals, he developed an aggressive habit of chasing anyone who came into his domain. Elisabeth took to carrying a stick around with her.

On Sunday, January 25, two American Navy jets swooped over the island. There was no time for a fire, so we ran down to the beach with a "We Require Assistance" flag that Elisabeth had made. We already had a large "SOS" in the sand made of coconuts for such an eventuality, so Elisabeth placed the flag beside it. Then all of us, jumping up and down, waved our arms madly in the air. It's strange how one thinks they will hear us shouting, but all of us were screaming our lungs out. I suspect the pilots must have thought we were zealously friendly people, for they gaily waved back at us, dipped their wings, and flew away. From the air, the pilots obviously had no idea the *Miken* was disabled, and after a few days of anticipation, it became apparent they had not seen our message in the sand.

Life had to go on, however. When it was obvious that no rescue was coming, Ken started to talk about finding a way to get off the island. Dave had discovered a single drum of petrol. This got Ken thinking about the twenty-five-horsepower outboard motor he had had aboard the *Miken*. Ken later took some of the petrol to see if it would run the outboard engine - it did. We were to find another drum of petrol a couple of days later.

Ken and Dave then made a mount for the engine, and the following day, we decided to test it out in the calm waters of the lagoon and explore some of the other islands we had previously had no access to.

The men loaded the fuel and mounted the outboard motor. The ladies prepared a picnic basket for the trip.

In the calm waters of the lagoon, the *Miken* cruised with ease. We spent a lazy day on an island four islands away, northeast from ours. Diving from this island, we found some lovely pink "baby-bottom shells." I spotted the remains of a small ship off the coral drop but, frustratingly, it was too deep for me to explore without scuba tanks. Otherwise, we did nothing special; we just relaxed and had a fun day.

Exploring the other islands in the lagoon, before testing the outboard engine in the open sea.

On our way home late that afternoon, we decided to take a run out into the open sea outside of the atoll beyond the lagoon and try some fishing there. As expected, once outside the atoll, fish hit every lure we threw at them. It was pandemonium!

Just as we decided we had landed all the fish we could handle, the outboard engine sputtered and then stopped.

I noticed we were drifting quickly away toward the south, so I told Elisabeth to don a life jacket. If we couldn't get the motor going, I reckoned we would swim for it back to the islands, if the current allowed. I did not want to go adrift in the boat.

We three guys got busy trying to persuade the motor to start again. Engrossed in our task, we heard Elisabeth suddenly cry out, "Look in the water, look!"

We raised our heads to see the boat completely surrounded by sharks. In fact, the water was boiling with them. I had never before, nor have ever since, seen so many sharks in one place. They were mainly oceanic white (silver) tips, which have a reputation for being man-eaters.

Ken looked at me, smirking, and asked, "You gonna swim for it now?"

I looked at all the sharks in the water and replied, "No need. We'll walk!"

However, my flippant reply hid a real concern of going adrift in this boat, especially unprepared. I said we should try to catch some of the sharks for food, as they can be sun-dried, in case we couldn't get the motor going. So, while Ken worked on the motor, we all decided to try our luck.

There was one very large shark swimming between the other sharks. We took turns trying to catch him. I baited a rod with a slice of bonito and threw it in. The water splashed up in fury as the sharks raced for the bait, but a smaller shark reached it first. Then Ken said he wanted to try for the big one, but he also hooked a small one.

Dave came up next. He was standing about six feet from the end of the boat when the big sharks hit his bait. Dave literally took off! Pulled right off his feet, he slammed into the railings of the boat and doubled over. Fighting gamely, he held onto the rod and managed to right himself to finish the fight, but the other sharks, now in a frenzy, bit off his line before he could bring it in.

Thankfully Ken managed to get the motor going again, and we headed home.

Early the next day, Elisabeth and I went for a stroll to the beach on the far seaward side of the island. We came upon some turtle tracks leading to and from the sea. We followed the tracks to the foliage and scrambled on our hands and knees under some low branches toward where the tracks stopped before returning to sea. Using our hands, we dug away at the sand, where it appeared the turtle had made its nest. Our labors were fruitless. There were no eggs to be found. It was a good sign, though, so every morning afterward, I went to that side of the island to search for tracks.

Eventually, my persistence paid off. On one particular morning, I decided to go for another dive on that side of the island. I wasn't in the water long before I saw an enormous green turtle heading for the shore. I remained very still and watched to see what it would do. It left the water and went ashore. I waited until it was a fair way up the beach, then swam back to shore after it.

The turtle weighed about two hundred pounds, so I had quite a struggle to upend it. I then ran back to the camp and told everyone I had a turtle that was more than likely carrying eggs. I was raised in the African Bush, so harvesting and cleaning game was nothing new to me. I said I would dispatch and clean the turtle, but everyone had to agree. This time everybody did, as we desperately needed a change of diet.

If you are squeamish, then skip this passage. We were in a survival situation, and this is what happened, so I will not sanitize the telling of it.

I have cleaned many animals, but this was the most difficult I have ever done. I used the sharpened machete to cut the head off the turtle, which I cast aside on the beach. Taking a sharp knife, I then cut into the breastplate close to the back right flipper. To my horror, the flipper came up and pushed my hand away. I reasoned this was just the nerves doing that. Then I looked at the discarded head. The turtle's eyes were looking straight at me. I brushed that aside as my imagination. So, I got up to walk to the other side of the turtle, and I swear those damn eyes in the severed head followed me! I then cut at the breastplate close to the front left flipper, and *that* flipper came up and pushed my hand away. I looked back at the head, and sure enough, the turtle's eyes were looking right at me. No matter which part of the breastplate I cut into, the corresponding flipper would push my hand away, and no matter where I was, the turtle's eyes followed me. I screamed at the animal to die already! I picked up the head and threw it into the sea.

The animal was so heavy that it took me over four hours to quarter and carry the joints and sides to camp. The meat was some of the best any of us had ever tasted. We made four large roasts as well as steaks and stews, and even the liver was used to make a liver-and-steak pie. There was a substantial quantity of meat still left over, and none went to waste. I cut the meat into strips and made what we call in Africa "biltong" (salted sun-dried meat). I had made the salt by simply boiling sieved seawater in a bowl, which, when evaporated, leaves behind salt crystals.

The inside of the turtle shell contained a thick layer of greenish fat (from which the green turtle gets its name). We rendered down this fat and used it in cooking. I also recovered eighty-six, ping-pong-sized eggs. So as to not make the same mistake as past shipwreck survivors and deplete our food resources, I buried twenty-six of these eggs close to where we had found the first sign of nesting.

Later, when these eggs ran out, Elisabeth and I went searching for more turtle nests. In one mound, we unearthed 146 eggs. Ten were rotten and forty we reburied. Every egg we took was utilized. They are very sweet but don't rise like chicken eggs do but rather cook flat. However, we were able to enjoy luxuries such as a small homemade cake and some biscuits.

We had an agreement with Ken that, once a week, we three guys would row out and check on the *Miken* just to see that all was okay on board and that the mooring hadn't shifted. As I was the only one who could dive deep enough to the anchor, I would swim down to make certain the anchorage was secure while Ken and Dave surveyed the boat for any problems, such as leaks.

On one of these occasions, while I was down underwater, I noticed a decent-sized barracuda swimming to the reef. So, on surfacing, I called out to the guys on deck that I would swim back to see if I could spear a fish for supper. Dave asked to swim back with me and try his luck to spear a fish again. So, while Ken rowed back, Dave and I headed into the reef.

As we reached the edge of the coral cliff face, I spotted a pan-sized grouper disappearing into a small cave. Dave had not seen it, so I decided to have a go at it myself. When I reached the cave, the grouper was still inside. It was a difficult angle, and my spear didn't penetrate the fish properly. It darted into a crevice, taking my spear with it. Knowing full well that its wild thrashings would call every shark into the area, I swam after it into the cave. After a short struggle, I managed to dispatch the fish and head to the surface.

In the interim, Dave had spotted reasonably good-sized sweetlips fish. They are plentiful and good eating, so I gave him the spear gun, and he dove after it.

I watched as he dove below alongside the reef, took aim into the coral, and took a shot. He then surfaced next to me, saying that he wasn't quite sure if he had hit the fish, and that he had left the spear below in the coral. My line on the spear gun was fifteen feet, the gun was about three feet.

Dave, still holding the gun, just managed to get his head above water. I handed Dave my fish, and while he held both the fish and the gun, I dove down the line to the spear to check it out, Dave had made a perfect shot on the fish; it was dead. I worked it out of the coral and headed for the surface.

Halfway up, something materialized way out in the deep blue. Heading at incredible speed towards Dave was an unmistakable, blue torpedo shape I knew well. Mako shark!

I chucked my mouthpiece and screamed a warning. Dave hadn't seen the approaching danger at first, but later said when he heard me scream, he immediately knew there was a shark.

The normal procedure when two divers are confronted with an aggressive shark is to swim back-to-back (I watch your back, you watch mine) and flip slowly but steadily back to shore, always with the shark in view. This sounds okay while discussing this on dry land, but when a person meets his first real aggressive shark in the water, usually the first thing on one's mind is to get the hell out of there. Especially when the shark is a cheeky one, and this mako was cheeky, very cheeky.

So, it was not surprising when, upon hearing my scream, Dave pumped his legs and made for the shortest route home. Dave is a strong swimmer, and we were still attached to each other from the spear gun to spear, each of us carrying a fish, of which this shark seemed keen to relieve us of. There was only one place alongside this part of the reef where the waves broke on raised coral, and also the only place where there was bad visibility - a big no-no when followed by an aggressive shark.

Dave had his head down in the water, heading straight toward the area with bad visibility. I shouted at him to hold up, but he kept going.

The mako circled and then focused its attention on me. I watched it arch its back and drop its pectoral fins, a sure sign it was coming in. Then the quickest shark in the sea came at me with its ragged buckteeth open. I kicked out at the shark with my fins, and it darted away but turned and came again, repeatedly darting toward and away from me.

This time as it came toward me, I attempted to jab the spear at it, hoping to scare it off. But Dave kept pulling at the spear in my hand every time I tried to fend off the shark, so this did not deter it much. Each time, the mako got braver and came closer. I decided that, instead of waiting for the shark to come at me, I would act aggressive toward it. So, brandishing and pulling hard at my spear, I charged at the mako, blowing bubbles and gurgling obscenities as I went. This action certainly astounded the shark, and it skulked a little way off, obviously to ponder this.

So, I was given a reprieve, which I used to swim quickly toward Dave, who was now into the area with bad visibility. I shouted to him to keep away from the breaking waves, but he kept going. However, once in the murky water, Dave collected himself remarkably well, and when I caught up to him, he calmly asked, "Okay, what do we do? Can't we just go for it and swim through?"

"No," I replied. "Not a good idea. We need to see the shark and keep him off us."

Elisabeth and Nicole were on the beach, watching from the shore. They had heard me shouting at Dave, and so they ran down to the shore to see what was going on. We could hear the ladies screaming at us, and I saw them pointing wildly. I turned and saw a fin coming in fast, and a dark shadow passed close by. So, side by side, Dave and I swam away from shore out to the sea again, toward good visibility.

The mako was waiting for us, obviously determined to get our fish. I considered giving him our catch but knew from past experience this could cause problems with later dives. We kept the shark at bay by blowing bubbles at him, but he still followed us as we swam farther along the coral table to where there were no waves breaking. Mako sharks are an open water species, so I hoped that once we entered the shallow water of the coral, it would not follow - it did.

At one point, it thrashed its tail above water several times as if in anger, and then it came in so close I nearly did give up our fish to prevent being bitten. In waist-deep water, we scurried and flapped as hastily as the current would allow to the end of the old jetty, where we clambered out as fast as we could.

Jubilantly, we stood up, laughing and punching the air as we swore at the shark while it vigorously thrashed its tail again on the surface a few more times before turning and slowly cruising out to open water. We were lucky; this fish has the reputation of being one of the most ferocious sharks in the sea.

All of us were understandably pumped up and excited by this experience when we returned to the Clubhouse. Ken, however, was not happy when he heard what had happened. He scowled and asked once again, "Gordon, what the hell are we going to do if you're attacked by a shark?"

After this, the discussion once again turned to the possibility that one of us would get injured or become ill. Ken felt he would be responsible and now firmly talked about finding a way to get off the island.

Besides sharks, there was another danger in the water we had to watch out for: stingrays. There were numerous of these alien-looking, disk-shaped creatures, which can attain up to eleven feet across the disk. These rays would bury themselves in the sand until only their long whip-like tails were visible, and they would lay motionless, awaiting a fish to pass by. Therefore, there was a real danger of stepping on one. Their tails are armed with a barb similar to the head of a fisherman's spear, which is a series of reversed hooks along each side. Should anyone be unfortunate enough to be pierced by the barb, that person would face a dilemma in addition to the injury itself. As the barb has reversed hooks, it cannot be removed without tearing the flesh. The only alternative is to push the barb through and out the opposite side. These barbs are also venomous and cause severe pain.

When I was diving in the Caribbean, I heard a story where an elderly but experienced skin diver presumably speared one of these powerful creatures only to be speared in return. The old man, it would seem, was then dragged under by the ray and drowned, as he was later discovered floating at sea with a broken-off barb through his upper arm.

To catch a ray by line is quite a feat. A ray I had caught for a moment bent a hook (on which I had previously caught a four-foot shark) almost straight. I did manage to spear them in shallow water, though, but even then, I had to be careful because they would attack me each time. Their wings are delicious to eat, and the meat, when curried, is not unlike tender curried chicken.

On the night of Wednesday, February 4, we were enjoying such a meal with a small glass of arrack while discussing various topics. Ken picked up a barb of the stingray, which I had saved to use for a spear myself. Then, tapping the barb into the palm of his hand, he paced up and down and guided the conversation toward our plans for the future on the island. He said he was aware that Elisabeth and I were quite happy on the island and content to let the future take care of itself. Ken felt, however, that he had to find a way of reaching help and offer us at least the chance of getting off the island. He was also anxious that, sooner or later, one of us would need medical attention. The recent run-in with the mako shark had made him all the more conscious of this. "Even something like this," he said, holding up the stingray barb.

Since the day we discovered the two drums of petrol, Ken had been forming a plan in his mind. He presented this to us now.

The nearest place we could reach for assistance was the American Indian Ocean Naval Base on the British isle of Diego Garcia, two hundred miles south of us. You may recall that, on the day we tested the outboard engine during our picnic trip, I had noticed Ken trying to work out how fast the boat was drifting.

With this information, and while knowing the outboard's fuel consumption, Ken figured out there was just enough petrol left in the drums and tank to cover the two hundred miles to the base using the outboard motor.

You may also recall that when the motor had stopped outside the atoll, we had noted the boat drifted south—toward Diego Garcia.

Ken proposed to complete the wooden rudder and tiller as well so that if there should be a following wind, the jury square rigged sail could be brought into play and if needs be (to catch more wind in the sail) the fly bridge could be cut off and dumped into the sea. Ken also pointed out that the journey, for the most part, would be across the Chagos Banks. So, should the worst happen and the fuel run out, the *Miken* could be anchored there in the shallows of the bank and if that happened, he then figured they would be close enough to Diego Garcia to be within radar range, that sooner or later, the Americans must come and investigate.

I disagreed vehemently, to the point where we argued. In my mind, there were far too many ifs and buts in this plan. Our attempt to be the first to cross the Indian Ocean in a forty-foot single inboard motorboat was a calculated risk. I felt the plan to cross two hundred miles of open ocean in a disabled boat was a desperate attempt by Ken and had no chance of success. I disagreed that he had enough fuel for that distance. I also pointed out that in the open sea, even in moderately rough seas, the motor would be constantly cavitating, and thus burning half its fuel in the air.

Despite the obvious risk, Ken was confident there was a good chance of reaching Diego Garcia and was determined to give it a try.

Ken was adamant he was going. I was just as adamant that, this time, Elisabeth and I would not be joining him. Ken agreed immediately and said that, as he wanted the boat as light as possible, he also did not wish Nicole and Elisabeth to go along for that reason and also the obvious implications of danger on this journey. As I was the one providing most of the food, I would need to stay to take care of them.

Ken went on to say that he and Dave would attempt the journey. I looked at Dave and waited to see what he would say (as I recalled him saying he would never get back on the boat again). Dave just looked down and never said a word. I wondered if Ken had bullied Dave into this decision and was going to discuss it with him. Then it occurred to me that perhaps, after all this time being the odd one out on the island, Dave felt maybe he was ready to leave. So, I let it be.

After further discussion, it was decided that Ken and Dave would undertake the journey as soon as possible. It is said that insanity and courage are often on two sides of the same coin, and I believe that was the case in this instance. Those two men, by accepting and taking on this challenge, had me both admiring their bravery and damning their stupidity.

By now, Elisabeth and I had come to consider Île Du Coin as our home and were happy to remain for the foreseeable future. Nicole never offered any opinion either way but seemed to accept that she would be better off staying with us on the island. Once again, though, I was a little concerned about her now being the odd one out, as Dave had been. As it turned out, there was nothing to be worried about.

Three days before Ken and Dave were due to leave, we celebrated my birthday with a half bottle of whiskey. We had a delightful, jocular evening, which continued late into the night. After that, it was early nights to focus on preparing the *Miken* for the journey. Elisabeth and Nicole organized the food supplies, enough to last the men at least ten days. Meanwhile, Ken, Dave, and I worked on the boat. Ken wanted as much off the boat as possible to lighten the load, which he hoped would help with the fuel consumption. I understood this but was not happy about their food and water supply. I came up with a plan.

Most of the coconut palms were high, which made getting coconuts from them quite difficult. However, I had previously found one palm loaded with green coconuts that were easy to reach. As this was a source of both food and water, I asked everybody to leave the coconuts alone on that particular tree in case we ever became desperate. Everybody had agreed.

Now I pulled Elisabeth and Nicole aside and proposed we cut down all the coconuts from this palm, and without Ken or Dave knowing, sneak the entire bunch onto the *Miken* and stow them below deck. This would give them a good supply of food and water for some time, and I figured the extra weight was a worthy trade off. Both Nicole and Elisabeth agreed that this was a good idea.

The weight of the coconut bunch, I have to say, was quite a bit more than I had bargained for. While Ken and Dave were busy working on the rudder, I slipped away, pushed the dinghy off the beach, and rowed to where the ladies were waiting for me with the stash of coconuts. We thread a branch through each bunch and, with the ladies on one side and me on the other, struggled to carry the heavy coconuts to the dinghy. Once we filled it up, we rowed out to the *Miken*, where we off-loaded all the coconuts onto the boat and hid them below. I would tell the guys about the stash just as they were leaving.

Tuesday, February 10th the big day arrived. Dave and Ken said their farewells to Nicole and Elisabeth. There was an uneasy quiet between us. I joined Ken and Dave in the dinghy, and we rowed out to the *Miken*. The ladies waded into the lagoon behind us and waved their last goodbyes. When we came alongside the *Miken*, we hauled the dinghy on deck and secured it. I tried not to show my concern as we shook hands, and I hugged my two friends. I told them about the coconut stash, and then dove overboard down the bow rope to release the anchor. When it had been pulled aboard, I swam alongside the *Miken*, waved, and wished them "the best of bloody British" in my best affected British accent.

"Let's hope it's the best of bloody Yankee!" Dave called back.

Ken gave me a thumbs-up, then turned the boat about, and they slowly chugged south of the atoll. I swam back to Elisabeth and Nicole, who were standing on a sandbank in the shallows. Together, the three of us stood silently and watched the *Miken* head slowly across the tranquil water of the lagoon toward the open sea, and finally disappeared. We didn't know it then, but a few miles south of our atoll, powerful easterly currents awaited their coming.

Alone on a Deserted Island with Two Ladies

Later, when back in civilization, some journalist salivated over me being *alone with two women on a desert island* and wanted to know all the sordid details. My response to them was always, "It just means twice as much nagging, pal!" and left it at that. Those reporters seemed more interested in our relationships than our survival. One newspaper report had as its headline, **"Romping Nude on a Desert Island!"**

I am sorry to disappoint anyone and will clear that up from the start: It was a nonevent in that regard. The three of us got on exceptionally well together and did most things as a team. However, there was no orgy or threesome. We respected each other's privacy, and every evening, after spending time together at the Clubhouse, retired to our own homes.

Alone with the two ladies. Cleaning at the water's edge.
Note: The raft at its moorings, Miken and the dinghy gone.

Nicole did often go ala naturel, Dave on a few occasions liked to go naked when he was alone, as did Elisabeth on a few occasions in private, and when the guys were gone, Elisabeth discarded her clothes more often and especially liked to swim naked. There was a day earlier on when Elisabeth and I had walked alone, naked on the far side of the island, this however resulting in our tender midriffs getting painfully sunburned. There was an occurrence a couple of weeks after the guys had left when Elisabeth came to me and said her period was quite late. I have heard that woman who live together often experience that their menstrual cycles sync, for later that day, Nicole informed us that she was also late. I had visions of us being rescued sometime in the future, me alone with two ladies and two babies, and a lot of explaining to do! However, to our relief, both ladies were soon regular again. So sorry if it bursts those journalists' bubbles, but there was no romping as the article implied, or as some of those reporters wanted to sensationalize.

At first, there was a strange atmosphere about the island now that there were only three of us. Nicole would often stare out to the sea toward the south.

"I know the supplies we gave them should be enough, but I wish they had taken more," she said. "But now it's too late."

By now, we were well organized and reasonably comfortable. Our kitchen was functioning perfectly, and our lounge was clean and cozy. We did still need to clear the fast-encroaching jungle, though.

Let me demonstrate how fast this encroachment could be. One morning, Elisabeth placed a stick approximately three feet long against one of the pillars of the shed, where it remained for the rest of the day and through the night. The following morning, she called our attention to the stick. Within that short time, a vine had already entwined itself halfway up its stem. Despite this, our respective houses were as livable as they could be. We now had two showers on the island (Ken had fixed one up), both with full tanks of water. The chickens had settled well, and we were still getting a steady egg a day. The maize crop in Daves' garden was flourishing. The fruit trees we had cleared of vegetation rewarded our efforts with a small supply of oranges and limes. I still had work to do felling trees, clearing bush in the grounds around our house, and maintaining the paths, but the only thing that really needed doing was obtaining food for our survival. We now did this together. Elisabeth or Nicole often gave me a foot up the breadfruit trees or helped to steady the long pole and hook to reach a juicy, rare orange. On occasion, they even joined me on my fishing expeditions but never on my spearfishing excursions, which would always invite shark activity.

Climbing for Breadfruit.

It was not all work, either. We raised two sets of goalposts, approximately twenty yards apart, in the waist-deep water in front of the Clubhouse. We had found a polystyrene float that had washed ashore, so we used it as a ball and played water polo, man against ladies. These matches were in serious need of a referee, as I believe there were more fouls in five minutes' play than there were in the chicken run, the ladies taking unfair advantage by ganging up and ducking me underwater every chance they got. Great fun, though! When it cooled down in the evenings, we would also play badminton in the partial shade behind our bungalow. Here, a couple of wild donkeys seemed to be getting used to our presence and liked to watch these games from the edge of the jungle.

Speaking of the donkeys, we did consider catching one, but as they were very wild, we weighed that up against getting injured. In the tropics, infection always has to be taken into account, so we decided to see if they would come to us eventually.

One morning, we noticed a school of dolphins playing in the water just off the edge of the coral in the lagoon. We donned our diving gear and swam out to them. Disappointingly, by the time we had reached where they had been, there was no sight of them. This, however, was to be the first of many a dive we enjoyed in each other's company together, either for shelling or just for the sheer pleasure of it.

One day, Nicole, who had never dived before coming to the island, joined me on one of my underwater photographic

184

expeditions, as I had my underwater camera with me. We swam to the outer reef, where just off into the deep, we spotted a giant barracuda eyeing us, seemingly fearless of our presence. They have a rather undeserved bad reputation of attacks on man, and I have often hunted them. Nevertheless, they are a voracious and ferocious fish armed with a terrifying array of vicious fangs. They can move at tremendous bursts of speed and are known to kill fish just for the sheer lust of killing. I hold these marine predators in great respect, especially when I would come upon a fifty-pound monster like this one.

I did not have my spear gun with me, and the barracuda was showing an unnerving interest in our presence. It slowly approached us, gaping and showing its array of teeth. I wished to photograph the brute, but I was uncertain how Nicole felt about facing such a dangerous-looking fish. To my surprise, I found her not only calm but showing as much interest in the barracuda as it did in us. The big fish must have found Nicole's scrutiny and bold approach rather disturbing, for it suddenly turned tail and sped off at great speed. Perhaps Nicole was now really an island girl!

Elisabeth stayed behind on shore that day, as she wanted to prepare some fire torches. She made these by binding old sacks to recently cut green sticks with old wire we had found on the island. That night, we placed the torches in diesel fuel, and when they were well and truly soaked, we removed them, carried them to the beach, and ignited them. Beneath the light of the torches, the three of us walked into the warm water of the low tide to explore the corals.

The sea becomes a different place at night as its nocturnal creatures come out from their hiding places. One of these is the lobster, which will stare, stupefied, in the light of the torch, and so it makes for an easy catch. There are also many types of shells that forage only at night, and we found some beautiful cones and helmet shells among them. Sea cucumbers were everywhere, which I knew were edible, but at this stage, I didn't feel the need to harvest any. Octopus, however, is very good eating, and although they are quite a job to clean and skin, the effort was always worth it.

Besides searching for seafood and shells, we also were able to enjoy the beauty of the marine life at close quarters. The variety of sea feathers and anemones, rich in many different colors gently waved at us to-and-fro from the current. "Sleeping" fish, especially parrotfish, could be approached cautiously, and even stroked. No matter where we went, each section of the coral garden had its own peculiar story to tell, and the library was endless.

When I think back to our time on the island, those moonlit nights are some of the most etched in my memory. If I were a painter, I would love to paint the picture I saw on those nights, which I will attempt to describe now.

The lagoon was so still that the moon cast a silvery glow on its surface, which shimmered every now and then, and rose up and down ever so gently, as if breathing in its sleep. I would turn to watch the two ladies, who, completely in their natural state, were wading naked under the friendly glow of their fire torches that reflected sparkles in the water around them. Each woman cut a wake in the still lagoon, their silhouettes casting their beauty against the backdrop of a palm-fringed beach behind them, on a small tropical island two thousand miles from the coast of Africa, far away in the middle of the Indian Ocean.

The next day, we all rose early and decided to go beach combing. We did this on the open seaward side of the island, as here, especially after a storm, is where any flotsam would most likely be washed ashore. We would find driftwood and/or plastic jars or containers of all sorts, but mostly we would find rubber sandals of different colors, sizes, and thickness.

We were later told that these sandals were an indication of an appalling tale. Apparently, certain factory ships had kidnapped children and went out into international waters, where the kids were forced as slave labor to make these and other products. Apparently, these discarded rubber shoes had floated hundreds of miles before being washed up on our beach.

On one beachcombing trip, we were amazed to find a perfect matching pair laying side by side just off the water's edge, almost as if someone had walked out of the water and slipped them off. Walking on coral tended to make short work of any shoes, so these sandals came in handy.

On one particular beachcombing trip, we had gone searching for one specific type of item: buoys. We found a myriad of these balls, common white polystyrene ones in red, orange, green, and blue plastic, and the decorative dark-green glass ones as well. I needed these buoys for a specific purpose: I had decided to build a raft. We needed a means to reach the edge of the coral reef and venture into the lagoon for fish. We also needed to keep our catch from the sharks, which were becoming more and more aware of my fishing and diving catches and were bolder each time.

I built my raft using a heavy door that I had removed from the entrance of the storeroom near the shed. The door was about seven feet long by about two and half feet wide. With the aid of rope and copper wire, I bound half the buoys we had collected to cover the underside of the door, leaving a gap in its center. Afterward, I placed a ten foot by nine-inch plank I had found washed up on the beach through the gap I had left in the center. Making certain the plank protruded out equally on either side of the door, I nailed and roped it into place. At each end of the plank, I tied a small buoy. These floats and the plank would be the raft's water wings (or outriggers) and hopefully act as stabilizers. Then I fashioned a set of paddle oars from one piece of flat wood by cutting away the middle of the wood equally on each side down to about three inches to form a handle grip, leaving about 1½ feet uncut at either end to use as blades.

Last, I found a long rope and a weighty block of iron to act as an anchor. I then dragged the door into the lagoon, buoys facing upward. In knee-deep water, I lifted the front end of the door, so it stood vertically on its back end, then with a slight shove, let it go.

There was quite a splash as the buoys and door hit the water. I winced, as I expected to see buoys shoot out in all directions from underneath the door as they took the pressure. To my immense delight, the door rose to the surface, then settled with all the buoys still intact and voilà! I had a raft!

The raft Sesame – Mark 1

I climbed gingerly aboard to see how the raft would take my weight. It wobbled slightly but supported me without much trouble. Jubilant, I shouted out to Elisabeth and Nicole to come and admire my proud workmanship. They arrived at the beach with a "What's that?" expression on their faces. I decided that trial was better than words, so I invited them aboard. The ladies waded out into the waist-deep water. Elisabeth climbed aboard first - we sank slightly, but the raft still held its own. Then Nicole climbed on.

The raft wobbled to the right, so we leaned the other way to counterbalance it. Then it wobbled to the left, so we leaned in the opposite direction. Alarmingly, one buoy popped out from underneath the front, followed shortly by another, then another. Pushed up by the buoys at the back, I watched in trepidation as the raft tipped on its nose, and with the help of our lurching weight, somersaulted head over heels and tossed us into the water. Spluttering, I rose to the surface to see two heads laughing hysterically among a colorful array of bobbing buoys.

Well, I was not about to take that kind of abuse, so I immediately set about readjusting the raft. The second version I presented to the ladies did me proud. Without a sign of struggle, the new raft held all three of us well, and on our maiden voyage, we paddled her more than a mile out to sea and back again without mishap. As the raft had now proved herself, we decided to christen her. As she obviously opened new doors to adventure, we affectionately name her "*Sesame*."

Elisabeth found a small rubber tube that had washed up on the beach and miraculously survived the reef. I found a piece of netting under one of the buoys, so I fashioned a hoop under the tube. Then Elisabeth took the piece of net and sewed it to hang under the rubber tire tube. I used this at times as a diver's buoy, which I would drag behind me when out diving for lobster, octopus, or clams. The tube and net were also used to trail behind the *Sesame* at the end of a rope whenever we went out to sea.

One of the Blacktip sharks caught off Sesame.

This came in handy, as there was not much room on the raft if all three of us wished to go along. One person could sit quite comfortably and be towed along on the outward journey until we reached a spot to drift fish off the end of the coral table on the lagoon side. The ladies really seemed to enjoy being rowed out to sea in their "carriage." However, the main purpose of the tube was to store the fish we caught.

When fishing in the *Sesame* out on the reef, we had a special procedure to follow. As the raft was barely long enough to hold the three of us, we either had to straddle her or sit sideways with our legs hanging over the side in order to be comfortable. Sharks, as I have mentioned, are attracted by the vibrations emitted from a fish in distress, so whenever one of us had a fish on the line, that person would shout "Legs up!" Then we would all raise our legs out of the water and sit with them crossed in the lotus position. One of us pointed out how ridiculous this must look to an onlooker, so it did not take long before the giggling started, which ascended into raucous laughter.

When a fish had been landed and killed, the surrounding water was thoroughly checked for sharks. Once all was declared clear, we would pull in the tube, where we would place the dead fish, then push the tube away and resume our positions to relax. "Up legs!" would often occur again before we were even comfortable. There were a few false cries, and someone would be forced to take a short dip. We always had fun and thoroughly enjoyed those trips on the *Sesame* together.

Strangely, although some sharks did investigate the fish in the tube, they never had a go at it. Part of me, though, thought it might have been fun if one of them did take us for a ride. I would hold the rope in anticipation, but the sharks seemed to be wary of the tube and left it alone.

Back from the lagoon after a day's fishing off Sesame.

The days that followed were blissful, but in the back of all our minds, there was a real concern for our companions somewhere out there in the Indian Ocean. It was not unusual to find one of us scanning the horizon. So much so that one day we realized that, without consciously thinking to do so, we had all shifted our chairs in the lounge of the Clubhouse to face the passage leading to the open sea.

On the day of February 17th, Nicole and Elisabeth were relaxing out of the midday sun in just this position. I had spotted a large trevally from the jetty and was trying to entice it to take my baited hook, when Elisabeth cried out to me from the Clubhouse. I couldn't quite make out what she was saying, but she was pointing excitedly out to sea. I turned and searched the horizon.

I immediately spotted what had gotten Elisabeth so excited. Way in the distance on the far side of the lagoon, I sighted a small white dot approaching. It had to be the *Miken*! Or was it? We decided to guard against becoming too hopeful.

It was possible for the *Miken* to have made the trip in such a short time but seemed unlikely, unless they had given up and were returning. I joined Elisabeth and Nicole at the beach, and we stood for what seemed like ages, watching the tiny white dot gradually grow larger and larger until it became apparent that it was the sail of a yacht and not the *Miken*.

A slight breeze was blowing, so the yacht made slow progress. Four hours after we first sighted it, the sailboat dropped anchor at almost the same place where Ken and Dave had hauled up the *Miken* anchor. A short while later, a tender lowered from the yacht and soon made its approach to the beach. The small boat beached in front of us, and two totally naked young Frenchmen in their late twenties stepped ashore, looking at each of us in total bewilderment.

As we welcomed them, one responded in broken English, "But dyu are peeepol!"

This is what they told us. They had crossed in their thirty-six-foot yacht from Djibouti on the east coast of Africa to an atoll east of ours, the Salomon Atoll (a small oval atoll consisting of eleven islets). As was the case with most yachts that chanced upon these remote atolls, they had chosen to go to the Salomon Atoll for the anchorage that was safer than that of Peros Banhos. They had been there for a few days and decided to visit Peros Banhos Atoll for a day or so. They knew from their charts that Île Du Coin was the main island, so they came directly across. One of the Frenchmen had been studying our island as they approached it when he noticed three small figures standing on the beach. He told us he had cried out to his companion, "Look! Zere is peeepole on ze beeech!" His friend brushed aside this ridiculous observation, declaring, "Imposeebol. Zose are donkeeeys!"

Here, I informed him flat out that it could not have been me he was seeing; it must have been the ladies. Laughing, he explained that he had made this assumption based on the fact that the main island in the Salomon Atoll had wild donkeys as well.

They went on to say that the man who first spotted us rushed down into his cabin, grabbed a pair of binoculars, then returned to the deck and focused them on us. Triumphantly, he had passed the looking glasses over to his friend, saying, "Look! Zey are peeepol!"

We were rather reserved when we first met the Frenchmen, perhaps because we had become somewhat protective of our island home, and frankly, we were not sure if we could trust them. My first question to them was whether they had a long-distance radio. They said they did not. I looked over at their new, state-of-the-art yacht and found this hard to believe but could not think of a reason why they would lie.

Much later, we were told that the reason they might have lied about this was because it was suspected by authorities on the Diego Garcia military base that they had stolen the yacht in Europe, and therefore, did not want to be traced for obvious reasons.

However, the Frenchmen proved to be charming, and so amicable that they soon won us over, especially when they said they would only stay for a day or so. They didn't seem to pose any threat to us.

When they had entered the atoll, they caught a good-sized red snapper, which they offered to us. With a few ingredients of our own, the ladies prepared the fish for supper that evening.

We had a pleasant evening with our visitors, but it was also rather strange. When we told them our tale of how we became stranded on the island, and that our two friends had gone for assistance in a disabled boat, the Frenchmen offered no help at all. (Again, it made sense later when we discovered they had perhaps stolen the yacht.)

I pulled Nicole aside and spoke to her about asking her countrymen to take her with them, as this would be her chance. However, I went on to say that Elisabeth and I felt it was rather strange that neither of the Frenchmen offered help, so we wouldn't ask and would prefer to stay on the island anyway. I also pointed out that if she went with them and once they got back to civilization, she could report the *Miken*'s attempt to reach Diego Garcia.

I cannot offer any reason for Nicole's response, whether she still held out hope that her boyfriend, Ken, would return, or if she felt she couldn't trust our visitors, but she flatly refused. Nicole did say, however, that she would insist they report on our situation as soon as they could. She then walked over to talk to the Frenchmen.

The two yachtsmen showed a lot of respect for "our" home and always asked if they could take or use anything on the island.

Two days after their arrival, they said they would be returning to the safety of the Saloman Atoll before resuming their sailing trip to the east. On their last evening with us, the Frenchmen said they had been very fortunate while in the Salomon Atoll. There, they had discovered a bottle of wine washed up on the beach with the seal still intact. They opened it, where, to their delight, it was still okay to cook with. With a magnanimously generous gesture, they used the wine to make us a luxurious turtle stew. After a great meal, we shared a little of our arrack with them and had an enjoyable evening in their company.

Before Ken and Dave had left for Diego Garcia, there was talk that, if they could get the *Miken* repaired there, they may call in at the Salomon Atoll on their return journey to look it over. As it was still too early for us to be certain that the guys hadn't made it to Diego Garcia, we told the French sailors there was an outside chance of seeing our boat there.

So, the following day, the Frenchmen left for the Salomon Atoll, saying they hoped they would see our mates there, and if not, they were sure our friends would soon return for us. However, they said the words without much conviction, and neither of them would look me in the eye as they said it. This left me with the distinct impression that they didn't believe it for a second. The whole visit, though a pleasant event, was rather surreal.

We watched as their white mainsail gradually grew smaller and smaller until, eventually, it vanished over the horizon. We were once again alone.

The morning after the Frenchmen had departed, I awoke to find my bed soaking wet; I was running with perspiration. This was not due to fever but simply caused by a stifling heat we hadn't experienced before. Elisabeth was sitting up in bed, fanning herself vigorously with an elephant ear leaf from a taro plant.

I walked outside to the veranda. There was not a breath of wind, the palms hung limp from the coconut trees, and the ground was distorted in a shimmering heat haze.

Elisabeth and I had a quick shower (which was all we could afford, as there had been no rain for a while). This refreshed us temporarily, but it was not long before we were sweating profusely again. That morning under the blazing sun, the three of us waded into the lagoon to try cool off, but it was like trying to cool off in warm soup. We swam out to deeper water, but even that didn't help much. I am used to hot weather, but after three days above 50°Celsius/122Fahrenheit in the shade, this became oppressive, even for me.

On the third day of this extreme heat wave, relief was finally on its way. Around midday coming over the horizon toward us from the east, a dark cloud mass was approaching from the far side of the lagoon. A slight breeze ruffled the palm fronds and gradually picked up to a noisy rattle. The heavens became darker, and on the far side of the lagoon, we could see white "horses" churning up the sea. The advance of the white-capped seas were approaching at an alarming speed. We were obviously in for an almighty storm.

A seventy-foot palm tree wrenched from its foundations and crashed into the ground, announcing the storm was upon us. The wind howled through the shed and plucked up our table and chairs in the Clubhouse. We felt a certain excitement in the atmosphere of the storm, for we ran laughing about in the wind and cooling rain like children at play as we attempted to catch our furniture fleeing into the jungle.

The arrival of the refreshing storm after the three-day heatwave.

Then the full might of the rain came pouring down in a solid sheet of water. Within minutes, two extra forty-five-gallon drums were overflowing.

Despite the soaking of our Clubhouse and some wind damage, we were glad for the rain and the drop in temperature. However, I hoped to hell that Dave and Ken were not out at sea in this storm with just an outboard motor and that they were safely anchored in Diego Garcia.

The storm passed that night, leaving our lounge and kitchen in shambles, so we had a lot of work to do to clean up the mess. Other than that, over the next few days, we only did what needed to be done and spent the time easily. These days began to mount up steadily. Each day's passing faded softly on the eye in glorious sunsets each evening as the three of us searched another empty horizon for any sign of our friends out there in the open ocean, which now edged towards being overdue.

We tried to reassure each other that perhaps the boat was taking longer to repair than expected, or maybe Ken and Dave were enjoying a friendly chat with the Frenchmen in the Salomon islands at that very moment.

The days turned to weeks, and with still no sign of the *Miken*, there came a time when we finally had to accept that she was now long overdue. We no longer muttered halfhearted reasons for Ken and Dave's failure to return. There could only be one explanation: they had obviously not made it to Diego Garcia, and by now their food and fuel supply must have run out.

This does not mean we gave up hope for them. Far from it. If anyone had a knack for getting out of a sticky situation, it was Ken. And with Dave beside him, they would be far from licked. Still, of course, the ocean didn't care either way.

During the course of each day, we continued to gaze along the horizon, hoping. We also became acutely aware of any unusual sounds, and perhaps at times our imaginations created a few.

An extract from the journal reads:

We keep on hearing noises; we rush down to the beach but there is no-one there.

One night, the radio suffered terribly from a static noise, as if a racing car (Doppler effect) was passing back and forth past the island. We have no idea what caused the sound.

An all-too-familiar sound crowed at first light one morning. Cocky was demanding to be released from the chicken run. I sat up grudgingly, stretching the cramp from my muscles. Elisabeth was already up and about, and when seeing I was awake, informed me that she was going to prepare breakfast before I released the "menace." She had to pass by the chicken run on her way to the Clubhouse and was in no mood for a run-in with Cocky. Before she left, Elisabeth reminded me to bring the mosquito net along with me when I came for breakfast. I assured her I wouldn't forget to do so, as we needed the net to execute a plan, we had discussed the previous evening.

Recently, along the shoreline every day at high tide, a large shoal of sardines passed by, herded by small blacktip sharks that were feeding on them. We decided there were enough sardines to go around and that the blacktips would not mind if, with the aid of the mosquito net, we attempted to catch a few for ourselves.

So, after breakfast, we kept an eye out for them, and sure enough, just as the tide was about to turn, the sardines appeared. There were thousands of them in one solid black mass, moving as though they were a single organism. We ran down the beach to get ahead of the shoal, then waded into thigh-deep water. We stretched the mosquito net between Elisabeth and myself while

Nicole attempted to shoo the sardines into it. The sardines moved in unison and stopped right in front of the net. Then the black cloud changed shape as it moved to go around us.

Blacktip shark herding sardines.

Well, we shooed, coaxed, pleaded, rushed at them, pounced on them, and swore at them. Nicole joined us at the mosquito net, which was now becoming soggy and heavy, not really fit for the purpose. The sardines enthusiastically joined in the spirit of the game and began running in circles about our ankles. Laden with a soggy, cumbersome mosquito net, we attempted to turn with them, and the faster we turned, the faster they circled. As this was not in any way productive, we got smart and, on cue, decided to turn in the opposite direction against them.

The sardines, bless their souls, enjoyed this different maneuver immensely and promptly turned with us.

Even the water polo games were never as strenuous as this one. After twisting, turning, stumbling, and falling over backwards, we eventually gave up, dragged the sodden mosquito net out of the water, and collapsed on the beach, exhausted. We didn't have a single sardine to show for our efforts.

We were not given long to feel sorry for ourselves and had barely caught our breath when the three of us suddenly bolted upright and listened intently. The second we realized what we were hearing, we were spurred into action. Coming our way was the unmistakable sound of an approaching airplane! We had rehearsed it more than once. We all knew what to do.

Nicole dashed about, grabbing at coconuts, driftwood, and short sticks to fill in an SOS we had made there some time ago. I ran to the raft.

Elisabeth bolted to fetch the "We require assistance" flag she had made and lay it beside the SOS in the sand. It was, perhaps, too late for her to throw greenery on the fire to make smoke, but she managed to find some. She chucked it on the burning coals in the kitchen, then ran back to join Nicole on the beach.

I paddled as fast as I could on the *Sesame* out into the lagoon, hoping to give someone in the plane a greater chance of spotting me.

As the sound of the plane drew nearer, Nicole and Elisabeth waited tensely on the beach. Coming unseen from the opposite side of the island, a propelled US Navy plane suddenly appeared over the top of the palms and roared over our heads. Jumping up and down, the girls waved their arms madly at them. The plane kept going and passed me just overhead in the lagoon. I waved my paddle furiously at them. The plane then dipped its wing and turned back towards us. We cried out in delight - they must have seen us! It passed over us again, then circled the atoll and flew off in the direction of the Salomon Atoll.

We were jubilant! Surely, we must have been spotted. Help would soon be on its way, and at last, we would get a search process underway for our two friends, who by now we were certain were lost at sea. The thought even crossed our minds that Ken and Dave might be aboard the plane. I was a bit concerned, though, that there was not more of an acknowledgment from the plane, but, as the girls were so excited, I kept that thought to myself.

However, the days passed, and it became apparent we were wrong in our assumption that the plane had spotted us. No one was coming.

We settled back into our life on the island.

A few nights after we had seen the plane, the temperature dropped to just below 28°Celsius/82.5°Fahrenheit, which was cool enough to sit around the fire. We found that in the tropics, one becomes sensitive to the slightest drop in temperature, and eight degrees was quite a drop. We had finished our supper and were relaxing, listening to the world service over the radio.

There is no denying that living on the island was about as far away from civilization as one could get, and the only link we had to the outside world was the radio. This fact was emphasized that night while we listened in silence to the world news broadcast.

I distinctly remember feeling as if I were a spectator watching a game of which I had no part. Like most spectators, I would probably make a poor referee, and it is all too easy to sit on the sidelines and pass judgment. Nevertheless, the human being is an animal of powerful thought, and be they right or wrong, we all develop a set of values by which we believe the game of life should be played. I am no exception.

What we heard over the news that night is immaterial. Just let it be said that at that moment in time, it showed the world events to be, in my view, a very sad place, and I felt I was not missing much. Here on the island, the only real problem I had was sharks, which that night sounded tame to me in comparison to the menace that seemed to lurk in different forms beneath the very foundation of our civilization. The pros and cons of each existence can, admittedly, be strongly debated. Living in civilization has its obvious advantages (which, believe me, are far greater appreciated on a desert island) than living in the wild does, but, I wondered, does living in civilization make us civilized?

But that was how I felt: wild. And although we were not totally carefree, mainly due to our concern for Ken and Dave, we did have a certain freedom that was a joy to experience. Some I would dare to say, (like Ken did for instance) would find the island to be almost a prison.

However, Elisabeth and I believed we were living a dream on our own tropical island, once described as an emerald necklace misplaced by the gods. For us, it was, indeed, pretty close to paradise.

The next morning, I awoke bubbling with a renewed vigor and energy. I still wanted to clear some bush around the house, but I hadn't felt the urge in the past few days. I had a hasty breakfast and wasted little time in getting stuck into the job. The rain was pouring down, which I found was the best time to work, as it was pleasantly cool. Elisabeth must have been caught up in my enthusiasm, because she soon joined me to give a helping hand. Completely naked, in pouring rain, in the grounds of our own house on our own island, we worked together. I have seldom, before or since, felt as content as I did then.

That night, as if to celebrate that day, we had a fireworks display. Elisabeth and Nicole were down at the water's edge, cleaning some pots using the beach sand, when I heard Elisabeth cry out in delight. I joined the girls at the beach to find Elisabeth dancing about in the shallow water. Every step she made, the water around her sparkled in a million brilliant lights. I bent down and cupped some of the bioluminescence into my hands, then tossed it into the air, the result was spectacular. On seeing this, Elisabeth and Nicole followed suit, and, laughing merrily, we tossed and splashed the illuminated water into the night sky. Eventually, the slight breeze of the evening began to chill our soaking-wet bodies, so we returned to camp and stood with our backsides to the fire: a perfect end to a perfect day.

We had many happy days like this, spoiled only by moments when we stopped and wondered about the fate of Ken and Dave. Nicole was naturally more affected by this, and there were times when she would gaze out to sea for great lengths of time.

The next few days, while I was fishing or working in the grounds of the house, Elisabeth decided to brighten up the Clubhouse. She dug out and collected the bulbs of three types of flowers she found on the island. Although they were similar in appearance to lilies, I have no idea what they were. Two had differently shaped flowers but were a similar snowy-white color, while the third had a lovely soft, red bloom. Elisabeth planted these around the perimeter of the Clubhouse.

Early one morning, while she was busy with her garden, I went fishing from the jetty, hoping to catch a shark on my shark-rigged hand line. Up to that point, I had considered sharks as mindless eating machines. Something was about to happen to change my mind.

I had caught some small fish for bait on my light line and waited. It was not long before a five-foot blacktip shark appeared. I baited my shark hook and cast it ahead of the shark. He went straight for it, and the fight was on! It took a while, but I managed to bring the shark close to the jetty, when it suddenly twisted and pulled the hook free, then swam off.

I had to wait some time, when eventually I saw the same shark approach again. I quickly baited my hook and cast it out into the water, where I could clearly see him approach the bait once more. This time, however, when the shark saw the dead fish, he darted around it to avoid it. I was amazed the shark had learned this, as that showed reasoning. But this was not the end of it.

Sometime later the shark returned, and I tried to tempt him again, with the same result. What happened next, though, made this event even more amazing. I spotted a five-foot nurse shark approaching, so I left the bait in the water to see if he would go for it. Sure enough, he went for it, when out of nowhere the blacktip shark came at great speed and rammed into the nurse shark.

At first, I thought the blacktip was fighting for the bait, but it showed no interest in the dead fish at all. It seemed more determined to keep the nurse shark away from the hook. I couldn't believe what I was seeing, but there was no doubt that this was exactly what the blacktip was doing. Over and over again, the blacktip rammed the nurse shark, trying to keep it from the bait. I called to Elisabeth, who was still tending her flower garden, to come quickly and see what was happening. The thrashing of the two sharks made such a cloud of sand, coral, and debris that, at one point, I could hardly see them. Then, out of the cloud, the determined nurse shark finally pushed past the blacktip and took the bait.

I fought the shark for some time when it suddenly dashed for a head of brain coral and wrapped the line around it. We were at an impasse, for I could not pull him in, and the shark was stuck around the coral head. So, before the line snapped, I called Elisabeth to come quickly and take the line. I had made a spear, which lay on the jetty, so with Elisabeth holding the line, I waded out to the shark with my spear as quickly as I could to try and dislodge it.

I found the shark with its body bent halfway around the coral head. Drawing my spear, I thrust it at the fish. The shark's hide is leathery and very tough, so the spear hardly penetrated, but it did manage to shift the shark. It shot away from me, unwrapping the line about the coral as it went. I shouted a warning to Elisabeth that the shark was running with the line.

Elisabeth, however, contradicted this, and replied that there was no fish on the line, as she was pulling in only slack. This was true enough, though the reason she was only pulling in slack line was because the shark had dashed off in her direction. I shouted back at her that the shark was still on the line. She assured me in turn that it was not.

"It's on, it's on!" I yelled back at her, moving as quickly as I could in the water to get to her.

"Gordon, it is gone. Look!" she shouted, holding up the slack line to show me.

The shark then suddenly changed its direction and sped away from the jetty, taking the slack in the line with it. The next part of our discourse went something like this:

"Gordon, there's no fish on this line!"

"I'm telling you, he's still on!"

"Gordon, I have the line in my hands; I tell you, there's nothing."

"I can see the bloody shark; hold on to the line, hold on!"

"Gordon, there's naaaah . . . Gordon, it is! Gordon! Gordon! Gordo-o-o-o-on!"

I watched as Elisabeth, her arms outstretched before her, tottered like a Chinese maiden in short, quick steps toward the edge of the jetty, trying to break herself as she went.

I reached Elisabeth just in time to prevent her from being wrenched off the jetty and towed away to sea; she obviously had no intention of letting go of the line. Elisabeth insisted she wanted to finish the fight herself, so as I held her, she battled a while longer, and after great effort, eventually landed the shark. With wife safe, dry, and smiling proudly, we headed back to camp with her prize.

We talked about how the blacktip shark had unquestionably tried to help another shark, even a different species, and still could not quite believe what we had seen. But on this occasion, instead of keeping our potential meal, this event moved us to release the nurse shark back into the sea.

A few days later, I went diving alone off the reef into the deeper water, where I spotted an octopus. As I dove after the creature, it released a cloud of ink in my face and headed for the shallows. There is no creature on Earth that can camouflage like these cephalopods. Not only will they change their color to suit the surroundings, but they also change the texture of their skin to match each part of the coral they are on.

This one did not get away from me. I headed back out to the deeper water with my catch in hand, but this time it was not a shark that approached me, but the graceful spotted eagle ray. It kept swimming as if in flight around me, perhaps because of the octopus catch I had, so just for fun, I decided to swim with it. The two of us danced together in circles as it "flew" in the water just beyond me. There were to be other occasions when I didn't have a catch with me, and this same eagle ray came and danced in circles with me. I even got disappointed when he didn't show.

I was still trying to get out to the dolphins, and at times, got close enough to see them, each time hoping they would get used to me and that their natural curiosity would eventually get them to come and investigate me. In the deep water, they would pass far below, blowing bubbles up at me, but they never approached any closer.

The seaward side of the island was the best place to spear big fish but was also teeming with sharks. Although the reward could be sizable, the risks were probably just as high. I also had to time my dives on this side of the island with the tide to avoid backwash currents. I waited for a low tide and went out alone to the open sea.

Once I reached the deep water, I could see large pelagic fish cruising past, but most were too far out for my comfort to follow. Fighting any speared fish out there would be pointless, and maybe even dangerous. I was tempted by a large wahoo that came into view, when just beyond the fish, an enormous hammerhead shark materialized out of the blue and cruised by, which quickly changed my mind.

So, I restricted my dive close to the edge of the coral cliff drop-off, and there, I eventually spotted a hunting party of "karambezi" (trevally fish) coming toward me. These are, to my mind, one of the tastiest fish in the sea, but they are also aggressive and powerful fish that move at great speed. (Giant trevally are known to attack sharks by ramming them with their bony heads.) I dove down thirty feet to be just below them as they approached.

I managed to spear a decent sized one. I have caught bigger ones, so I was taken by surprise when this fish shot off, almost jerking the spear gun out of my hands, - and the fight was on! I knew I had to subdue it quickly due to the sharks, but this fish had other ideas and pulled me down. I hadn't been able to surface for air, so my lungs were beginning to ask for it, but I held on. Perhaps it's somewhat of a competitive edge in me, or the fact that I could not afford to lose my speargun, but I wouldn't let go. Soon, my lungs were not just asking for air but begging for it. I scanned the area, and sure enough, two gray reef sharks were approaching fast.

I thought, *Oh hell, game over!* Fortunately, the approaching sharks actually worked in my favor, for the karambezi also spotted them. It sped to the surface away from the sharks, then towards the shallow water of the reef - and me with it! At the reef's edge, I managed to grab the trevally by the tail and lift it out into the shallow water, where I stood, gasping for air with my prize in hand. I stood watching as several reef sharks passed close by in the deep-water drop-off just a few meters away from me.

Karambezi (Trevally) speared on the seaward side of the island.

As I waded to the beach in the low tide, I remembered that Elisabeth and I had an excursion planned for when a particular event coincides with this tide and sunset, as that is the best time to catch a fish that the author Zane Grey had eulogized as one of the greatest light tackle game fish for its size in the sea, and is sought after by anglers all over the world. I had seen several shoals of these fish in abundance in the shallows, some of which were the biggest I had ever seen.

After Elisabeth had landed the nurse shark, she now fancied herself as something of an angler and wanted to try her hand at catching another fish. So, I planned this excursion together to try and catch some of these bonefish just for the sport of it. This fish I would catch and release, as they lived up to their name for being very bony, so I preferred other fish for the table.

As stated, the best time to catch these bonefish was when a low tide coincided between the late afternoon and sunset.

We had to wait a few more days for this tide to correspond perfectly.

The night before this day arrived, we celebrated our eightieth day on the island with the last of the arrack we had. I was down to my last two cigarettes. I smoked half of one for the occasion and put the other half away for later.

Ken and Dave had now been gone for seven weeks. I suppose we now should have accepted that only the worst could have happened to them, but strangely, we all still held out hope they would appear one day.

When the day of the bone fishing expedition arrived, Elisabeth combed the beach and collected a bunch of hermit crabs, which we were to use for bait. It was another beautiful day, with perfect conditions prevailing. The sea was still and calm.

That afternoon, Elisabeth and I collected our gear, then waded to where the *Sesame* was moored in the lagoon to prepare the raft for sunset fishing. We were standing in such a way that we both faced a small island, which lay about five miles south of us and was the last in the line of islands before the passageway that led out of the atoll.

At the same instance, we both noticed a rather strange phenomenon occurring on that particular island. Its palm trees were only just discernible against the strikingly blue sky, but it was these palm trees that had captured our attention. Instead of swaying to-and-fro in the breeze as usual, they were moving horizontally to the left of the island. Then, to our absolute astonishment, the island itself grew longer right before our very eyes.

We stared in amazement until, eventually, at a very gradual pace, the new growth divorced itself from the island. My heart missed a beat as I realized what it was. In disbelief, Elisabeth and I stared at it, not daring to say a word lest we be deceived by some evil trick of light to only have the apparition disappear. But it did not disappear. What we had watched pass behind the island into full bold view were masts behind the palm trees giving the illusion of moving palms and then the growth was the full bulk of a huge U.S. Navy armaments ship.

We vaulted onto the jetty and madly waved our arms about. A few questions passed between us: Why were they here? Were they just passing by? Would they stop? Had they seen us? Were Ken and Dave perhaps with them? Nicole was soon by our side and joined in our excited gesticulations. Just as I said we must quickly put greenery on the fire to make a smoke signal, Elisabeth spotted a tiny orange dot entering the lagoon from the ship. It was coming toward us! Rescue was on its way.

I said to Elisabeth, "Looks like we have some visitors. Let's put the pot on the fire and welcome them with some citronella tea, coconut milk, and some of the jaggery."

"Good idea," she replied excitedly, and ran to put the pot on.

Rescued!

The dinghy sped down the outside of the reef, then came in around the old jetty and made its way toward us. It carried three men, who were all wearing bright-orange life jackets.

Nicole cried out, "It's Ken and Dave!"

We quickly realized, however, that was just wishful thinking; it was not our friends. The dinghy ran up the beach, and the three men jumped ashore. The first man to reach us held out his hand, and with great gusto, introduced himself.

Our rescue party.

"Nigel Wells, British commander, Diego Garcia, can we be of assistance?"

I think he expected we would be half starved and desperate for water, for after we introduced ourselves, Elisabeth said, "We have the pot on; would you gentleman like to join us for a cup of lemongrass tea?"

The British commander's jaw dropped in unabashed astonishment. Totally flabbergasted, he stuttered a few um's and ah's, and then responded, "Ah, um, yes, well, thank you very much, I would be delighted!"

Before anything further was said, we asked straight off the bat, did they have any news of our friends and the *Miken*? We waited hopefully as the Commander, unfortunately, confirmed our worst fears and told us our friends had not made it to Diego Garcia. The naval base had also not received any report or word on their fate.

The two men who accompanied the Commander were a junior British officer and a marine of the US Corps.

Relaxing out of the sun in our cane chairs, enjoying our citronella tea, the Commander told us how and why they had come to be here.

On Diego Garcia, the Commander had received a report from one of the US Navy planes that a yacht had been sighted anchored in the Salomon Atoll.

The existing charts of the Chagos Bank are old and not very reliable; hence no Naval vessel had visited these particular waters before. It was decided on Diego Garcia to send out the ship to these seas for the first time and investigate the yacht in the Salomon Atoll.

The naval ship followed the outer, deeper water of the Chagos Bank which would take them to the Salomon Atoll. When they arrived outside the archipelago, they said the yacht they had spotted from the plane was still anchored inside the lagoon. The Navy ship was too large to be taken into the lagoon, so the Commander went in using the dinghy. Once ashore, he was met by the two Frenchmen we had met, and he spent a while ashore with them.

The Commander said the Frenchmen were very standoffish and did not offer up much information about themselves. They did say they had been to this atoll some weeks ago but needed supplies and had sailed off to Sri Lanka to stock up and had just returned.

So, obviously, the Frenchmen had not reported on our situation.

The Commander looked about at our setup and was not stingy with his compliments. He said he was impressed. He also prided himself on being very strictly environmentally conscious while on Diego Garcia, and these islands fell under his jurisdiction. He went on to say, however, that he was not impressed at all with what he saw on the Salomon Atoll, as apparently, he found trash and rotten fish strewn all around the island there, with no order at all (he said they had even noticed human feces floating up on the beach). The Commander said, because of this, and other reasons he would not elaborate on, he stamped the Frenchmen's passports and gave them a week to leave the islands.

(Conversely, later on, the Commander offered Elisabeth and me sanction to return to Peros Banhos Island if we wished to do so, and even offered us a post as caretakers with full support, supplies, radio etc.)

The Commander Nigel Wells said they spent the entire day on the island in the Salomon Atoll and, at first, the Frenchmen said not a word about us marooned on Peros Banhos, or our friends who had gone for help in a disabled boat. Nigel said it was only as they had made their farewells and stepped into the dinghy to return to the ship that one of them walked up and asked if the two guys in the motorboat had made it.

When the Commander inquired who he was talking about, the Frenchmen replied, "Well, two months ago, we found these three people stranded on an atoll west of here" and went on to tell some of our story.

Nigel said he was furious they hadn't mentioned this until the last minute.

The British Commander immediately reported this to the Captain of the Navy vessel, who, without hesitation, exclaimed, "Two months ago! We're going in for them; let's hope they're still alive."

And so, the big ship diverted from its homeward course into the Chagos Bank archipelago and came to our rescue.

Commander Nigel seemed to pick up very quickly on the fact that we considered this island our home and were now somewhat protective of it. I have to give him credit, because he was very sensitive to that.

We had hoped every day for aid to come to us, but now it was here, Elisabeth and I felt we did not wish to accept it. We had come to love the island dearly and had grown to consider it our home. The thought of leaving it now appalled us. We realized our concern for being found had stemmed from our wish to find our friends. So, our discussion turned to this, and we said we couldn't speak for Nicole, but Elisabeth and I wanted to stay on the island for the foreseeable future.

The Commander looked about him and said again how very impressed he was with the way we had organized ourselves and survived our eighty-two days on the island. He could well understand that we may have second thoughts about leaving it. However, he pointed out that if a proper search was to be arranged for Dave and Ken from Diego Garcia, it would have far greater impetus if we were there to give it support in person, and if necessary, ensure its further organization.

However, he was not averse to having someone on Peros Banhos atoll. We discussed the logistics, even to the point of making a helicopter pad somewhere on the island. However, that could be discussed later. Right now, we would have to make a decision whether to stay or leave, especially as there was not much daylight left, and the ship had to return to base. (The Commander said it was costing a fortune just for the ship to be here.)

Elisabeth and I figured the solution was obvious, as Nicole would want to return to civilization, and she could make the appeals for a search for her boyfriend Ken, and our friend Dave. Elisabeth and I, then, would remain on the island. To our bewilderment, when Nicole heard this, she said that if we don't leave the island, then neither would she, and she preferred to see if Ken and Dave would return.

We pointed out that, after seven weeks, it was highly unlikely they would return, but still, Nicole was adamant: If we didn't go, then neither would she.

To this day, I do not understand this decision, but it put Elisabeth and myself into a dilemma. So, the two of us took a walk together to discuss this. Elisabeth pointed out that, as the Commander was sanctioning our stay on the island, we could always find a way to return later. (According to Nigel, the fact that I was born in Rhodesia, which made me a British subject, would work in our favor, as these were British territory islands.)

I was still trying to think of a way to stay when we returned to the rescue party. I informed the Commander I needed the night to make up my mind, and that I could not just get up and go. Aside from our parting from the island, returning to civilization also needed a little while to accept.

The Commander reiterated that the ship had to return to Diego Garcia, but he would talk to the ship's skipper via his walky-talky radio. Surprisingly (even to the Commander) but gratefully, the Captain said he understood and would drop anchor. So, the US Navy ship waited the night for us.

For a while, we had been threatening to cook one of our chickens, so we invited the Commander and his men for supper. They declined graciously and said they would return in the morning for our decision. To be honest, I believe the British commander was just being tactful. He knew that one way or another, we would have to leave.

We never did have the heart to kill any one of the chickens. I left one of the showers dripping into the concrete bath below the tap, so they would have sufficient freshwater. There was certainly enough feed for them to forage. Perhaps someday in the future, someone would be grateful for them, or perhaps they would just flourish undisturbed. (Years later, we were to hear through the yachtie grapevine that our island was the place to go to hunt down wild chicken.) Despite the lack of chicken that night, we had a feast and opened the canned fruit we had saved.

Elisabeth and I still were undecided when we rose out of bed early the next morning. We walked down to the lagoon, sat on the palm-fringed beach, and surveyed our island home, we were loath to leave.

After some discussion, we knew we had no choice. We had to return to civilization and set in motion a search for Ken and Dave.

It would not be possible to take all our supplies and furniture, as there would be only enough room for our personal belongings in the dinghy. As a result, we did not have much packing to do. Despite this, we kept putting off the packing as though we were trying to prolong the final hours. Eventually, we trudged off and laboriously packed our cases.

I walked over to Cocky and his brood, opened the door to the chicken run for the last time, and tied it back. I found and collected three oranges from a tree full of still growing fruit; it wouldn't be long before these trees were smothered by the jungle again. I then walked past Daves' garden and picked our first, and last, maize cob. The banana tree Dave had planted would have made him proud, could he have seen it. (Even my tree was looking good.)

Nicole and Elisabeth met me at the Clubhouse, where we had a light breakfast, then waited for the dinghy to arrive. We had not waited long before we saw not a dinghy, but a launch coming in for us. With this revelation, we quickly gathered and packed our now-extensive shell collection, as now there would be enough room to accommodate them. The launch anchored off the coral reef, the dinghy was lowered, and the same three men came ashore.

The Commander wished to have a quick look about the island before leaving. On his tour, he noticed Dave's banana plant and asked if he could take it back to Diego Garcia, as they had none growing there. It struck me how understanding this man was by asking permission. It was also good to know that Dave's effort would at least benefit someone.

Further on our walk, we came upon the old, quaint little church. Commander Wells was quite taken by it. We entered to have a look around. Inside, he found, to his delight, the waist-high statue of St. Joseph. The figurine was in need of slight repair, but the Commander knew someone on Diego Garcia who was able to do such repairs. So, he once again asked us permission to take the St. Joseph statue back to Diego Garcia and present it to the American priest at the base.

A few days later, when he presented the statue, he did so unknowingly on the clergyman's birthday. The Chaplin informed the Commander that St. Joseph was, in fact, the patron saint of American Navy pilots, and that the day Commander Wells had removed the statue from the church was none other than St. Joseph's Day.

We returned once last time to the Clubhouse and carried some of our belongings down to the beach to load into the dinghy. The rest I loaded onto the *Sesame*. I will admit, I was quite pleased and proud of the fact that my raft carried just as much, if not more, than the dinghy. The Commander remained behind on the beach with Elisabeth and Nicole, while his two men took the dinghy to the launch and off-loaded our gear. Then, with me as her proud skipper, I paddled the *Sesame* on her last voyage to the launch, where the rest of our gear was hauled aboard. Then I rowed back towards the beach and tied my raft for the last time at her mooring. I often wonder if she is now broken up by heavy seas, or still floating patiently in the shallow waters of the lagoon, awaiting my return.

Elisabeth, Nicole and I then swam from our beautiful island that had been our home for the past eighty-two days. The Commander decided to join us on this final mile or so swim out to the launch. As I swam out ahead on my own, I spotted a familiar shape below me in the clear water. It was "Granddad," the hawksbill turtle, following me out. I turned on my back and called out to Elisabeth, "Look who's come to say goodbye!"

As I was given a hand up by one of the two sailors who had remained on the launch, they welcomed me back to

227

civilization. One of them remarked on the fact that I had an underwater camera with me and inquired if I had managed to take any underwater shots. I replied in the affirmative. He then asked if it had occurred to me that I was most probably the only person to have ever photographed the underwater life on the corals of these islands. It was a strange fact to consider and suddenly made my rolls of film my most important possession. Although, later, we discovered some of the films were damaged, but a few of them were okay. So, at least I had captured something of our time here on Île du Coin to take away with us.

The other marine asked if I would like some water. I thanked him but said that we had water on the island. He asked then, "Yeah, but do you have ice water?"

"That, we don't have, and that, I won't say no to!" I responded eagerly.

That's something else taken for granted in civilization. On the island, all of us would often fantasize about the dew running down the glass of an ice-cold drink. As I assisted the ladies out of the water, I told them the guys had ice water.

"Yes, please! Yes, please!" was the immediate response.

We slowly sipped the ice water, savoring every drop, and then turned to look at our small paradise that had been our sanctuary and home for the past eighty-two days. The finality of it hit us, and a quiet sadness descended on us. I noticed a few tears on Elisabeth's cheeks. Nobody said a word.

A sad farewell to our island home.

The anchor was raised, the launch fired up, and the three of us stood together and watched, sadly, as our beautiful tropical island became more and more distant.

The day was Thursday, March 19th, 1981: One hundred and two days after that fateful morning we had all set out from Trincomalee to attempt to cross nearly four thousand miles across the Indian Ocean in a single-engine, forty-foot motorboat, the *Miken*.

Approaching the Meteor.

The huge armaments ship, the *Meteor*, loomed before us. On approach, a large gathering of people waited on the stern deck. Nigel got on his radio, and soon, the large crowd disappeared, he must have figured we were not yet ready to face that. A smaller group was waiting at the stern launch drop that had been lowered to receive us. The launch slightly rocked and lurched as we were helped from its deck by the sailors. Once aboard the ship we were met by clicking cameras, warm handshakes, shouts of "Welcome back to civilization," and a fusillade of questions.

Rescuers offering helping hands.

The Commander, still considering our adjustment, realized we were not ready to thrust ourselves back into the jaws of civilization, so without being impolite, he took us directly to our cabins to settle in. He said he would be back later to take us to meet the Captain, who apparently was anxious regarding our health and could not believe we were physically well.

There is an interesting point I would like to make here: When we had realized we were stranded on Île Du Coin, we adjusted to the requisites of island life very quickly, whereas when we returned to civilization, it took us weeks and weeks to readjust, even the noise and the hustle and bustle of the ship got to us.

Later, we were taken up to the bridge by our rescuers where we met the Captain and assured him that, other than a few coral cuts and bruises, we were in good health. We then joined the officers in the mess hall and enjoyed some of the pros of civilization: steak, pork chops, turkey, fruit salad, and the castaway's dream—ice cream!

Interestingly, though we all enjoyed the sumptuous meal, none of us could eat much of it - though that could not be said of the ice cream!

After the meal, we joined the Captain in his cabin and enjoyed an ice-cold beer. I am not a heavy drinker, but the dew from an ice-cold drink that we had often reminisced about on the island was now actually in my hand. I wondered if I would ever take that and many other things for granted again.

While we enjoyed the beer, the Captain and the Commander warned us to be cautious of any optimism regarding the search for our friends. They pointed out that the *Miken* had been lost at sea for almost seven weeks now, and that the Indian Ocean was a vast, practically empty expanse, surrounded by countries with few or no facilities for extensive sea-search operations. They said Diego Garcia itself could only search an area of about four hundred miles within its vicinity. The Captain also informed us that just south of Peros Banhos, there were not southerly currents as we had believed when the *Miken* had drifted that way on our excursion using the outboard engine outside the atoll. He said this was most probably just the flow from the lagoon. He also said further south, there were, in fact, powerful easterly currents, and that there was no way the *Miken* would have gotten through. The skipper went on to say our friends most certainly would be at the mercy of those currents (even with a sea anchor or drogue) and would drift rapidly toward the Sumatra seas. He also pointed out that, being adrift for such a long time, there most certainly would have been some storms, and in big seas, a motorboat without a keel, and with just a four-foot draft that had no power to keep its nose in the wind would most certainly flounder.

At that point I was still hopeful, so I responded to the Captain that Ken was as tough as they come, and with Dave by his side, if anybody could survive, those two would.

The Captain countered this with, "I applaud your optimism, but you need to be realistic. The sea will drown a tough guy just as easy as a weak one."

I could not argue with that. But at that stage, the girls and I still clung to our hope.

After conversing with the Captain a while longer, he excused himself and called a seaman to escort us to the ship's stores to find us some (in his words) decent clothing. This was how we were introduced to the hospitality and generosity we were to experience during our stay with the 29 British and 2,500 Americans on Diego Garcia. In my travels, I have seldom experienced anything to compare with their kindness and help.

We slept fitfully that night, as we could not get used to the unfamiliar noises of the ship. The following afternoon, we docked in the Diego Garcia archipelago naval base. As we disembarked from the launch onto the pier, we were met by the American Commander, and the British commander's lieutenant.

Nigel - the British Commander, and his lieutenant, Stanley, became our immediate hosts. Stanley had our supplies (and seashells) loaded into a jeep, and then we were driven to the "officers' country," where we received what could only be described as VIP treatment. We were given our own air-conditioned rooms, and after which, the ladies were taken to the hospital for a thorough medical and dental checkup. I politely declined this offer, as I felt I did not need it. The woman returned to the officers' quarters with new lead in their teeth, patched up, and declared fit.

We were met by a television crew, who asked us for an interview. We nervously, but gladly, agreed to do so. I figured we could use this platform to further our appeal to search for our two friends lost at sea. Once our faces had been recorded for posterity, Stanley announced we had better feed those same faces. He led us to a white-clothed table shining with silverware, and we were served a meal par excellence. With our appetites satisfied; and liqueurs, spirits, and beers produced; American officers arrived, and a memorable evening was in the making.

One of the American officers asked if we would like to see some slides of the islands on which we were marooned that had been photographed from an aircraft and went on to say how beautiful they looked from the air.

I have been undecided whether to relate this part of our adventure, as we were so warmly welcomed and treated so kindly by all the people we met, but it is part of our story.

We gathered in a room with all the big brass from the marines, Navy and Naval Air force, both from the American and British contingents, along with some men from the press.

The slides were projected onto a screen, where indeed, the photos showed Peros Banhos beautifully from the air, and we could now appreciate why they had once been described as an emerald necklace lost by the gods.

We watched as the fourth slide came up, whereupon Elisabeth jumped up and cried, "Stop, wait, look there!" She pointed at the slide on the screen. "There's us! There's Gordon on the raft, there is the SOS in the sand. Look, there's me and Nicole!"

And, sure enough, there we were! We had been photographed, obviously by the US Navy plane that had passed over us on the island. There was a deafening silence as I felt the embarrassment descend on the room. Even I cringed for our hosts. For their sakes, part of me wished we hadn't seen the slide.

After the slideshow (which had prematurely ended), the top brass informed us that planes had been sent out to search for the *Miken*, and that signals had been sent to all the various major ports in the Indian Ocean and surrounding shipping lanes. Once the various authorities had seen them, a Seabee was assigned to bring me the responding signal sheets.

We were invited to stay on Diego Garcia for a few days to see if they could come up with any results before we left for whichever mainland we were to be flown to and then organize a search from there. One officer informed us that we were only the second civilians ever allowed to stay on the base. (The other was an elderly solo sailor, who had tropical sores so bad that they were getting gangrenous. He was successfully treated on Diego Garcia and sent on his way.)

The signal sheets started to arrive sooner than I expected. Each time the Seabee sailor arrived with them; I saw by his demeanor what the response would be. The signal sheets piled up one after the other. Negative, negative, negative...

The following morning, we went for a dive, after which we were chauffeured around the island by Stanley and generally kept entertained. We had been trying to keep our hopes high, and we constantly assured each other good news would come.

But when we returned to the officer's quarters, a pile of new signal sheets waited for us—all were negative. We waited for more sheets to arrive, but after a while, they dried up. No more were forthcoming. I think our hosts were very understanding and patient with our constant inquiry regarding more signal responses.

One officer then approached us and said we should prepare ourselves, for what he said was the inevitable, as all signals were now answered. The officer also said that for seven weeks adrift, there should be some news either way, good or bad.

He reckoned it was more than likely that the *Miken* must have gone down.

After that moment, I think the real seeds of despair were sown. I believe we made poor company for our hosts.

Nigel could see the change in us and decided to try to lift our spirits.

That night, at the invitation-only British pub, Stanley organized a barbecue and general get-together. Two officers picked us up that evening to drive us to the pub. Before we left, Nigel said he would see us there later, as he had something to attend to.

The British pub had a wonderful atmosphere. Someone was playing a piano, people were singing pub songs, and there were darts and a pool table to entertain. The men in the pub tried desperately to cheer us up; however, we found it difficult to reciprocate their cheerfulness, as we were now morally exhausted. We sat down quietly at an empty table, each of us in our own thoughts of Ken and Dave. At about nine o'clock that evening, Nigel arrived at the pub and called for silence. He had a sheet of paper in his hands. When he had everyone's attention, with his face deadpan, he read from the paper in a monotone voice, without a trace of emotion, as though he were reading a funeral sermon. This is what he read:

Greek tanker, Gherestos 3.50 South 2.15 east. Found disabled boat Miken registered Male Maldives .stop.

Here Nigel lifted his head from the signal sheet and at the top of his voice read out aloud:

Ken Oulton, British, David Faulkner New Zealand, Stop.
Survivors are in good condition stop!
Drifting for seven weeks stop!

They had left February the 10th in the uninhabited Isle Du Coin, Perros Banhos Atoll Archipelago. stop.

Three persons requiring assistance, stop
Mr and Mrs Gordon and Elisabeth Brace British and Miss Nicole Hascoet French stop.

Proceeding near Diego Garcia on 13 knots. Master.

The bar crowd roared in cheer. No matter how hard I tried, I could not contain the tears running from my eyes. Elisabeth and Nicole came running into my arms. Together, we cried and laughed in sheer joy and relief.

"Now, where's that beer!" I shouted.

The next day, by consulting the sea charts, we discovered that the Greek tanker had found the *Miken* adrift on one of the main shipping lanes, approximately 750 miles due east of Peros Banhos. It took the tanker almost two days to cover that distance.

As the signal sheet ended with "requiring assistance," and then naming the three of us, it was obvious the guys did not know that we had been rescued as well.

On Monday, March 23, a Navy Patrol boat went out to meet the tanker which was too large to come in close to the islands. Stanley drove Nicole, Elisabeth, and I to the most northern part of the island, where we waited, watching for the patrol boat's return. After what seemed an age, we at last sighted the patrol boat coming into the atoll, and there on tow behind her was the *Miken*. All of us jumped into the jeep and raced down to the pier. We arrived as a navy launch was already on its way to meet the patrol boat. The launch came alongside the patrol boat, but we couldn't quite make out who was climbing aboard. The launch then cast loose and turned toward the landing pier, where we all waited. And there, standing head and shoulders above anyone else, his arms raised high in a "Here we are" position above his head, was Ken, and standing shyly beside him was Dave.

US Navy launch bringing our friend's boat back safely to us. Note: Ken standing head and shoulders above the rest waving in the distance.

As the launch came alongside, and before the boat even docked properly, Ken leapt across to the pier, with Dave not far behind him. Ken swept up all three of us in his huge arms.

An emotional reunion caught on camara.
Note: How thin Ken and Dave are.

At last, the moment that may have never been: We were all reunited.

As Ken embraced us, I noticed tears rolling down the rough sunbaked face of the big man, and they don't come much tougher than him.

The moment that may never have been. Our reunion captured on American television.

Even though one would think they didn't have much weight to lose, Dave and Ken both looked a lot thinner (they each had lost around fourteen pounds), but in spite of this, and considering their ordeal, appeared fit and well. Ken was in high spirits; Dave, however, seemed quiet and subdued at first, but gradually, the Dave we knew was telling us about their seven weeks adrift at sea, and asking how we survived. We all returned to the officer's quarters, and this is some of what they told us.

After they left us from Île Du Coin, they had made for the Chagos Bank, which they crossed to with relatively few problems. Leaving the banks, however, they were met with rough seas, which caused the small motor to cavitate repeatedly, thus giving the boat little or no thrust. When they realized they were losing the battle, they debated whether to keep going for Diego Garcia, or try to return and find anchorage at the banks. They decided to try and return. However, they hadn't realized just how far east the currents had pushed them, and they ran out of fuel before they could return to the banks.

Using the canvas from the square-rig sail, they fashioned a sea anchor to try and remain in the area, hoping a plane from Diego Garcia would spot them. No plane came, and even with the drogue the *Miken* quickly drifted east. So, they decided to raise up the canvas and allow the boat to drift into the shipping lanes with the hope of encountering a ship.

They drifted for days, and their food supply soon ran out. However, fish, especially Dorado, are attracted to debris floating in the sea, and they will often sit underneath or beside any flotsam they can find for days on end. This was the case with the *Miken* drifting, so Dave and Ken were able to gaff some fish from the side of the boat and haul them aboard. Ken, Dave, and I all come from rugby-passionate countries, and Dave said his rugby skills came in handy as he tackled the flapping fish on deck. Some fish stayed beside the boat for a good length of time and became quite well known to Ken and Dave. Each morning, they would rise to see that Charlie was still there, and so was Fred, and Dick, and so on. One Dorado they had gaffed and landed slipped out of Dave's arms as he tackled it and escaped back into the water. This fish didn't swim off, as would be expected, but reassumed its position beside the boat. It was easily recognized due to the gaff wound on its back, and despite its harrowing experience, the fish stayed with the boat for a while.

Any fish they had caught and didn't immediately eat was cleaned and then dried in the sun to be kept. They supplemented their diet of fish with a seagull that had been unfortunate enough to land on the *Miken* and be caught by Dave.

For water, they cleaned out their forty-five-gallon fuel drums, and when the chance presented itself, filled them with rainwater.

Ken said they blessed us for the bunch of coconuts we had stowed before they left the island, declaring they were lifesavers.

After a few days adrift, Ken and Dave painted a large SOS on the deck of the *Miken*. Ken discovered one battery was just strong enough to light up a spotlight he had with him. Eight ships went by, ignoring all their SOS signals. Even flares they had sent up were ignored. One Greek tanker actually stopped and asked them what the problem was, then tossed them a parcel of food into the sea, which Dave had to paddle after by using his surfboard. Then the ship just continued on its way, without even bothering to report the boat in distress.

The Captain of the tanker who finally did stop and come to their aid was furious when he heard that a fellow countryman of his had behaved in this fashion. However, he, too, had been cautious when he found the *Miken* drifting helplessly. Before the

Captain of the *Gherestos* allowed Ken and/or Dave aboard, he interrogated them extensively, shouting down to them from the deck of the ship through a hailer. Even then, he allowed only Ken to come aboard at first, while the tanker crewmen trained fire hoses on him.

The Captain explained later that he had reason for his precautions. Apparently, the seas in that area are badly troubled with piracy, and just a few weeks prior to finding the *Miken*, the tanker itself had been pirated. The Captain also mentioned the "boat people" refugee problem, which ships were not prepared to deal with.

I have always had the impression, other than when at war (and at times and even then) that men at sea obeyed a timeless law to assist fellow sailors in distress - a brotherhood that never ignored a cry for help at sea. It would seem this is but a fallacy in these seas, which appears only in the lines of poets or in the compassion of individual men such as the Captain of the Greek tanker *Gherestos,* who also went out of his way to bring the *Miken* close to Diego Garcia. So, our sincere thanks go to that Captain. Once Dave was allowed to join Ken on board the ship, the Captain gave Ken the choice of either using his onboard crane to pull aboard the *Miken*'s engine, then let the motorboat drift away, or to take the chance of towing the *Miken* behind the tanker. Ken decided on the latter. He said for most of the journey, he sat astern the tanker, anxiously watching his boat being towed behind the tanker at an alarming rate of thirteen knots. After forty-nine days since leaving Peros Banhos archipelago islands, the *Miken* finally made it to Diego Garcia.

I am in no position to give a full account of Dave and Ken's experiences during those forty-nine days; I can only imagine what it must have been like.

Considering the speed at which the *Miken* was towed, she fared the journey well, and surprisingly, only suffered superficial damage. The Americans generously offered to repair and attend to the boat to get her seaworthy again. They confirmed later that the huge storm we had survived just out of the Maldives bent the drive shaft. It amazes me that the wood took the pounding, but the metal shaft and rudder did not.

Ken was about to accept this kind offer when the American Commander said he had been looking for a boat such as the *Miken* to use for recreational purposes on Diego Garcia. He then asked if Ken would consider selling her. Should he agree to this, then we could all be flown to Nairobi in Kenya, as one of their planes made weekly scheduled stops in Nairobi anyhow. This offer solved some problems that Ken would have to face once he reached Africa with the *Miken*, so he accepted.

The Miken safely moored at her new home – Diego Garcia.
Note: The SOS on the foredeck and the battered flybridge.

Two days later, the British and American officers approached us, very embarrassed. They informed us that a new chief accountant, who had recently arrived on the naval base, insisted that we pay for our fares to Kenya. Although they had tried vigorously to change his mind, he remained adamant, we had to pay. The deal for the purchase of the *Miken* had not yet reached a final agreement. As for the rest of us, we needed the small amount of cash we had for when we arrived in Kenya. These people on Diego Garcia had been so kind to us that we knew they would have tried all they could. Nevertheless, we had a problem.

Then Nigel and Stanley suggested, "Why don't you sell your shells as souvenirs to the military base personnel?"

We felt this was a great idea, and so, with the officer's aid, we began to organize it. Stanley was quite adept at sign writing, so he tried his hand at making some placards.

Two examples he penned to catch the eye were: "Sale of Shells" and "Pay a FAIR price for valuable FARE to help toward our FARES home."

That evening, tables were set up for us in the foyer leading into the American saloon. At first, the sale went disappointingly slow. I think most of the soldiers believed we were trying to con them, and they eyed us suspiciously. Some were blatantly rude, even to the ladies.

An American Military Policeman approached us politely and said he was intrigued by the unusual appearance of two ladies at the table of seashells and asked why we were here.

We briefly told our story and explained our predicament.

A sailor who had just walked in and overheard us said to the MP, "It's true; I've just seen them on the TV."

"You want to tell me that after all you've been through, that mean son-of-a-bitch wants to make you pay for your fares? That plane has to stop in Kenya anyway!" the MP roared.

He went on to say that he was sure most of the personnel didn't know our story. He told us to remain right where we were, then turned on his heels and stormed into the bar.

I believe our story must have been explained heatedly and then quickly spread among the clientele, because the military policeman hadn't been gone long, when men came out of the bar in steady numbers and bought up the shells. Even the few soldiers who had been rude earlier came and apologized, saying they hadn't realized our situation. Some men walked up to the table, deposited five or ten dollars, and then walked away. The ladies ran after them with the shells they were entitled to, but these men replied that the pleasure was theirs, no shells required.

After an hour or so of this, a group of marines approached us and asked if we now had enough funds, and if so, would we like to join them at the bar for a drink? The pleasure was ours. We had raised enough to cover our fares.

After a great night with a great bunch of guys, we walked back to the officer's quarters on somewhat unsteady legs.

The following day, a television crew set up an interview with Ken and Dave. During the interview, I was struck by something that Ken had said. The presenter asked several questions, then turned to Ken and asked him what their major concern was while they were adrift at sea?

I was expecting him to say water and food, or perhaps big seas and storms. But the big man replied that his biggest worry was the three of us who were left on the island, and the sharks I constantly had to face off.

Elisabeth and I were very moved by that sentiment, so what happened later that evening is hard to fathom.

To be honest, I hardly think it's worth a mention, but it is part of our story, and many since have asked how we all got along together.

One of the marines Elisabeth and I had met at the saloon asked if we would like a Diego Garcia T-shirt. We said we would love to have one, so he said he would send me one later.

That evening, there was a knock on the door to our living quarters. I opened it to find a sailor with an armful of T-shirts. I placed the pile of shirts on the table and chose two for myself, as did Elisabeth, then said that the others were welcome to look through the rest to pick some for themselves.

Dave looked at the one I had chosen and said he wanted that one. I said no, it was my choice. Dave then became extremely upset. I was taken aback at first, but then I got angry and I went back at Dave. He sat down and said he also didn't like how we were behaving with our hosts. I was astounded by this statement, as Elisabeth and I had been nothing but courteous to all the people on Diego Garcia. So, I asked him what the hell he was talking about and to give me an example. He couldn't come up with one, but responded it was not just himself who thought so, but so did Ken and Nicole as well. Ken was sitting down, and after what he had just said at the TV interview regarding his concern for us, I really got mad and flew at him in a rage, demanding he tell us what the hell we had done!

I think this must have looked comical, because I was standing while the big man was sitting, and we were staring eye to eye. Just as well, he did not stand up!

Ken said, "Gordon, this has nothing to do with me."

"Ask Nicole, then!" Dave called out.

I turned on Nicole and asked her, "What the hell is this all about! After all we've been through together?"

Nicole replied it was because she didn't appreciate that Elisabeth had asked to use the officer's washing machine, and then had broken it!

I could not believe what I was hearing. Elisabeth had used the washing machine, and it did break down, but it was certainly not her fault. This blowout we had was so petty, it obviously had nothing to do with the T-shirts or the washing machine. Analysts will be able to decipher it better than I can—I'm sure there's something Freudian about it. I mention it because it was one of the very few occasions when we had a petty argument. For the most part, we got on extremely well together.

This altercation was overheard by the officers in their rooms, so the following day, I went to apologize. To a man, the officers were very understanding. Stan said, "Gordon there really is nothing to apologize for. We think you handled it well; it's just emotions coming to the surface."

Elisabeth really is one of those people who gets on with everybody and is liked, and even loved, by everybody who knows her, so she was quite upset by this argument. As a result, the following day, there was undoubtedly tension between us.

That morning, Nigel announced there was plane leaving in the afternoon for Kenya that could take Dave, Elisabeth, and myself (Ken was still working out the final details for the sale of his boat).

We made our heartfelt thanks to all the big brass and officers of Diego Garcia, who had been so kind to us, with a lot of hearty handshakes. Ken also came and thanked us. He told us his brother was living in Kenya, and he had sent word to him that we were coming. Ken then asked us to stay in Kenya for a while with his brother until he and Nicole arrived, as he wanted to show us around before we left. I replied that I would like to, but if it took a while for him to wrap things up at Diego Garcia, we would not be able to hang around too long.

Nicole was nowhere to be seen.

Television cameras whirred away as we made our farewells to Nigel and Stanley at the airstrip. We were handed earplugs and then boarded the noisy C-130 aircraft. We took off from Diego Garcia on Wednesday, March 25th, 1981. We had spent five unforgettable days there.

Dave, Elisabeth, and I resolved the previous night's nonsense between us quite quickly, as though it had never occurred. I was sad we left without seeing Nicole and smoothing things over with her as well.

Our story had been sent from Diego Garcia marked "confidential" to our respective embassies. This we had asked for, as we wished our families to hear our story from us firsthand before hearing about it from the media. Somehow, though, the press found out, and only some of which actually interviewed us while many did not, with the result of some misleading articles.

This caused a serious problem when we arrived in Kenya, for, unknown to us, one newspaper article reported that five of us had been marooned on a deserted island, two of us went adrift on a game fishing boat and floundered, and only the three stranded on the island had survived.

Having read that article, Ken's brother and his wife came to the airport to meet us, so when we arrived on an unscheduled military plane, only the three of us disembarked and went through customs and immigration. When Ken's brother saw just Dave, Elisabeth, and I, he immediately assumed that one of the two who did not survive must have been his brother. Before we could clear the barrier and let them know Ken was coming later, he and his wife turned away, extremely upset, and headed for the door.

By the time we were outside the airport, they had driven away. Ken had given us his brother's address, so we found a taxi and drove out to his coffee farm, where we tracked him down. He apologized for running out on us, but then, still visibly upset, explained why. We assured him that Ken was okay, and the article was wrong, and that Ken would be arriving as soon as he had wrapped things up at Diego Garcia.

We had stayed on the coffee farm for a couple of days when word came that Ken and Nicole were on their way. On the evening of our third day in Kenya, at Ken's brother's request, Dave, Elisabeth, and I drove to pick them up at the airport. We were late arriving, so I dropped off Dave, who went to meet them while Elisabeth and I parked the car.

As Elisabeth and I entered the terminal of the airport, we saw down the hall ahead of us that Dave was already greeting Ken and Nicole. When Nicole looked past Dave and saw us coming through the doors, she ran screaming down the foyer toward us.

"You're still here! You're still here!" Tears were streaming down her face as she embraced both of us.

The five of us were once again together, and our friendship as strong as ever.

We contacted our families. My mother said she knows her son well, and then flippantly said she was not surprised and was never too worried. Dave and Nicole's family were very much relieved, as they had feared the worst.

In Denmark, Elisabeth's father had become extremely concerned as to our fate, as he hadn't heard from us for three months, nor had any confirmation of our safe arrival in Kenya. He made several inquiries to the Danish authorities, and eventually went personally to their offices to see if they could assist in locating her, or at least find out if anything had happened to us. The Danish officials hadn't been very helpful at all, so he told them, in no uncertain terms, what he thought of them and stormed out of their offices.

When our story hit the newsstands, Elisabeth's family were astonished to see a large headline in bold type on the front page of a major Danish newspaper, (translated to English from the Danish below) It read:

Besked til ængstelig far fra Udenrigsministeriet:

"VI HAR FUNDET DERES DATTER HUN STRANDEDE PÅ EN ØDE Ø"

Message to an anxious father from the Foreign Ministry:

"WE HAVE FOUND YOUR DAUGHTER SHE HAS BEEN MAROONED ON A DESERT ISLAND!"

END

Postscript

Since arriving back in civilization, Elisabeth and I did plan to return to our tropical island in the middle of the Indian Ocean. To further that end, sometime later, we purchased a thirty-seven-foot catamaran sailing boat in South Africa.

While we were stranded on Île Du Coin, I had discovered a spot where a catamaran could be brought over the reef with its low draft at high tide, beached on the island, and could also be refloated the same way. We would then not have to worry about the unsafe anchorage there.

Our catamaran was named *Zulani* after a Zulu legend, of a man known as the "Wise Wanderer," which my safari operation is still known to this day. Sometime later, after sailing the infamous South African coastline a few times, I tested the *Zulani* in the notoriously dangerous, Vasco da Gama yacht race, where she became the first catamaran to get line honors. I then felt we were ready, and shortly after that, we headed aboard the *Zulani* up the east coast of Africa.

We ended up spending three months sailing the Mozambique Channel, with some exciting adventures there. Instead, however, this set us on a different course. Those adventures are for another time, perhaps. So, we never did return to Peros Banhos atoll - not yet anyway.

Acknowledgements

It goes without saying that we shall always be indebted to Commander Nigel Wells and Lieutenant Stanley Goodridge.

Our special thanks also go to:

Captain Tony Peltz, USN Commanding Officer

Commando Paul Bennett, USN Executive Officer

Captain Camalich, all the officers, and CBS of USNS *Meteor* of the Navy Support Facility, Diego Garcia

About the Author

Gordon S. Brace was born in Northern Rhodesia (now Zambia) in 1954. He received schooling in both Rhodesia (North and South), spent a year in England, and then two years in South Africa. Finally, he completed his high school certificate in Rhodesia (now Zimbabwe). Following this, he was set to enroll in university to pursue a six-year dental science diploma. However, beyond his formal education, Gordon was fortunate to gain another form of learning in the African bush. At a very young age, he met and was mentored by an old white hunter and his superb indigenous tracker. Both individuals honed his skills in the ways of the African wilderness and nurtured Gordon's passion for the wildlife there. There was a time during his upbringing when Gordon spent an entire school term in the bush with these wilderness experts instead of attending school.

At the age of six, Gordon was introduced to the wonders of the tropical underwater world along the Kenyan coast and soon after that, the Seychelles and Mozambique islands. Gordon's mother encouraged his travels from the age of five to wherever her budget could afford. By the time Gordon left school, he had already extensively traveled across Africa and Western Europe. The prospect of spending six years at university and another three to four years establishing a practice in a profession he wasn't truly interested in didn't sit well with him. The allure of the whole world and stories of tropical islands with magical coral reefs, along with exciting wild places, beckoned him instead.

He packed his backpack, left the university behind, and headed for the warm waters of Durban on the eastern coastline of South Africa. There, he dived for lobsters, briefly joined a lifeguard club, then boarded an ocean liner for Europe, where his adventurous life truly began. Gordon has since traveled to more than 60 countries worldwide, mostly avoiding winters and chasing summers. He obtained his scuba diving certification while wreck diving in the North Sea but primarily sought out tropical reefs, from the Caribbean and Hawaii to the Red Sea, the Great Barrier Reef of Australia, the Maldives, Florida, and most of the Indian Ocean coastline and its numerous islands.

Gordon engaged in both recreational and professional diving. His mother later bought a fishing boat in Cape Town, South Africa, where she became perhaps the only commercial fisherwoman in the country at that time. Gordon joined her for a while, fishing and diving for abalone, gaining valuable experience handling an ocean-going motorboat. During this period, Gordon also had the opportunity to work with dolphins for a short time.

Gordon introduced Elisabeth, his young 19-year-old Danish-born wife, to Africa. She fell in love with the wild places there and was a perfect companion for Gordon's lifestyle. The two of them would soon establish their own safari business, organizing trips through all the Southern African countries for both photo and adventure safaris. When their daughter Che arrived, she practically grew up in a 4X4 Land Cruiser alongside a tent personally designed and equipped to serve as a bush home. Che would often run around naked and barefoot as a toddler, displaying total fearlessness amidst the surrounding wildlife.

Subsequently, Gordon and Elisabeth purchased a 37ft ocean-going catamaran named Zulani (after a Zulu legend of a man known as the 'wise wanderer'). This yacht became the only catamaran to achieve line honors in the infamous Vasgo da Gama yacht race. The sailboat led to numerous adventures, including a three-month sailing trip exploring the Mozambique channel and islands. Additionally, it was among the first yachts to sail up the Zambezi River (a potential adventure story for another time).

Later, Gordon managed and operated several hunting ranches, becoming deeply involved in African wildlife conservation and land preservation. This commitment eventually led Gordon and Elisabeth to purchase a ranch themselves in the Limpopo province of South Africa, which they also named Zulani.

This land, once used for harmful agriculture and cattle farming, was then restored to the wildlife that originally inhabited it. Over time, not only reintroduced wild game like giraffe and zebra roamed the land but also various creatures, including insects like dung beetles, diverse birdlife, reptiles, and several predator species from hyenas to leopards, which returned in healthy numbers. Their efforts also helped save the topsoil, allowing the indigenous flora to recover.

Gordon currently manages his game ranch in South Africa and organizes photo safaris, hunting expeditions, fishing trips, and dive safaris in all the neighboring countries. He continues to explore wild places and seeks out tropical dive spots worldwide.

Printed in Great Britain
by Amazon

37139870R00155